IDEAS IN MILTON

IDEAS
IN
MILTON

William J. Grace

UNIVERSITY OF NOTRE DAME PRESS
Notre Dame   London

PR
3588
.G67

© Copyright 1968 by
University of Notre Dame Press
Notre Dame, Indiana

Library of Congress Catalog Card Number: 68-12290

MANUFACTURED IN THE UNITED STATES OF AMERICA

CONTENTS

	FOREWORD	vii
I	THE HISTORICAL GENESIS	1
	Radical Protestantism Versus the Church of England	9
	Milton and Radical Protestantism	13
	Milton's Concept of Freedom	20
	Political Freedom and Natural Hierarchy	23
II	THE HUMANISTIC BACKGROUND	32
	The Millennial Idea	39
	Milton's Concept of Right Reason	45
	The Degree of Puritan Influence	50
	Milton as a Christian Humanist	56
	The Hellenic Influence	61
	The Theme of Glory	66
III	THE FALL OF MAN	72
	The Human Situation	81
	The Nature of the Fall	86
	The Justification of Providence	89
IV	THE IMAGE OF SATAN	101
	Satan as Ironic Hero	104
	Satan's Search for Glory	106
	The Consistency of Satan's Characterization	113
	The Critics and the Image of Satan	117

Ideas in Milton

V	IDEAS IN THE POEMS	124
	The Companion Pieces	124
	The Ideas of Moderation and Excess in *Comus*	130
	The Religious Vision of "Lycidas"	139
	The Images of Christ and Satan in *Paradise Regained*	146
	Samson Agonistes and Puritanism	152
VI	MILTON AS A POET	168
	Milton's "High" Style	176
	Milton's Poetry and the Baroque	180
	EPILOGUE	189
	BIBLIOGRAPHY	194
	INDEX	199

FOREWORD

THE FOLLOWING pages have a modest but, hopefully, a useful purpose. Their objective is to delineate the main complexes of ideas to be looked for in the reading of Milton, as an aid, especially for the undergraduate student, toward reclarifying and rethinking the questions that Milton, as an artist, perennially raises. The book is intended as a critique of the esthetic functioning of Milton's ideas rather than as a source study. However, it is the author's hope, as well, that some of the suggestions in the book will serve as a catalyst for intelligent readers coming upon a serious reading of Milton for the first time.

I am indebted to Professor Don M. Wolfe, editor of *The Complete Prose Works of John Milton*, for a sustained encouragement and an unremitting enlightenment in regard to Milton, to Fordham University for a faculty fellowship that permitted me the time to organize the material, and to Miss Joan Grace of the Fordham English Department for some of the most fruitful ideas and suggestions to appear in the book.

In any treatise on Milton a great deal of the material must remain in the field of opinion rather than of certitude. A personal point of view must inevitably appear at times in the following pages, which the author hopes will at least be helpful as a point of departure from which the reader may rightly disagree with him.

Ideas in Milton

The text followed in the poetry is that of Merritt Y. Hughes, John Milton: *The Complete Poems and Major Prose* (New York: Odyssey Press, 1957); for the prose, *Complete Prose Works of John Milton*, Don M. Wolfe, general editor (New Haven: Yale University Press, 1953–1966) Vols. I–IV, and *The Works of John Milton*, Frank Allen Patterson, general editor (New York: Columbia University Press, 1931–1938) 18 volumes in 21. The prose spellings have been modernized.

I

The Historical Genesis

THE SEVENTEENTH CENTURY is an age gravely concerned with religion. Its temper in this respect is very different from that of our own age. Many today tend to think of religion in rather general terms as a means of promoting good citizenship, giving a healthy moral tone to society, and helping to preserve integrity in the individual. But religious differences are not an overriding national or international concern. It is therefore difficult for us to realize the bitterness that developed among religious groups of the sixteenth and seventeenth centuries and the extreme violence of much of the controversy.

In the seventeenth century religion was actually a cause of civil war in England between adherents of the Established Church and what, for lack of a better label, we shall call radical Protestantism. Both groups regarded Roman Catholicism as their enemy, but since the Roman Church ceased to have any major political importance in England, it became a more or less distant bogeyman which all could lambaste for rhetorical diversion.

Ideas in Milton

It is helpful to have some idea of how the different Protestant theological perspectives arose, because this provides a key to many of Milton's concerns and to aspects of his work.

Radical Protestantism, in contrast to the Protestantism of the Church of England, originated in the Lutheran reformation. Luther was an Augustinian monk, and a great deal of his thinking reflected the views held by the Augustinians during the Middle Ages. The Augustinian order was in many ways the most influential of the four great orders and its centers were located in cities. It was not devoted to work among the rural poor as were the Franciscans and Dominicans or to the development of the land as were the Benedictines. If in speaking of influence we mean contact with the more prominent and wealthy members of society, the Augustinians had a special position. The Augustinian Friars (a mid-thirteenth century foundation) had not been founded by St. Augustine himself, but they followed certain rules Augustine had proposed for the religious life, and they regarded him as their patron.

Augustinian theologians placed heavy stress on grace as the central concept of their theology, and this fact was to have great historical importance. One of the major problems of sixteenth-century theology was the question of the relationship of grace to good works. Underlying this relationship was the question: What is the nature of man in terms of the context of original sin? St. Augustine's influence was particularly important on this matter. His thinking developed over many years, and in this one sense he is like the Plato he deeply admired: his intellectual life is not one of fixed positions. In order to understand Augustine's thinking on a particular matter, one must take an inclusive view of his whole range of mental development.

St. Augustine says of Adam and Eve that "the greatness of their crime depraved their nature" (*The City of God* XIII, ii).[1]

Men would not have died "had not the first two (the one whereof was made from the other, and the other from nothing) incurred this punishment by their disobedience: in committing so grave a sin, that their whole nature being thereby depraved, was so transfused through all their offspring in the same degree of corruption and necessity of death . . ." (XIV, i).[2] "Concerning man's first origin, our present life (if such a miserable state can be called a life) does sufficiently prove that all his children were condemned in him" (XXII, xxii).[3]

One of the most difficult words to define in or out of context is the word *nature*, and Augustine's "depraved nature" simply increases the difficulty. Philosophically speaking, nature can mean essence. Milton uses the word in this sense. Nature can also mean the whole of what something is, both its "essence" and its "accidents." St. Augustine uses the word to mean both essence and accidents, whereas St. Thomas Aquinas uses it to mean essence alone. In the late Middle Ages commentators on St. Augustine began to attribute to the word *nature* as Augustine used it the meaning of essence as Aquinas used it. Actually, the nature of something could be "depraved" in the sense that its accidents had been injured. Man could have lost a position in Paradise that related to his total nature without his essence being affected. He has real losses, but he remains essentially a man. Etienne Gilson, on this basis, makes a pointed distinction between what he calls authentic Augustinianism and Late Augustinianism; he finds Augustine and Aquinas in basic agreement if it is realized that Augustine means by *nature* all that man is (essence and accidents) but Aquinas means essence only.[4] Whatever the scholarly facts should have been, history shows that the interpretation gradually developed that St. Augustine maintained man was *essentially* corrupted through original sin.

In Thomistic thought it is assumed that the essence of something cannot be depraved without the nature of that thing being changed. If man's essence is affected through the Fall, man is no longer man, but something else. If we were to take a parallel from modern science, are we to consider original sin a mutation? We know that a man might lose his leg in an accident and sire a child who had two perfectly good legs. But if a man had only one leg because of a mutation, he would sire a child with one leg. The question is whether original sin is like the accidental loss of the leg or is it like a mutation? The Late Augustinians looked upon original sin in terms of a mutation.

Through such semantic relationships develops the sixteenth-century doctrine present in Lutheranism but made more explicit in Calvinism, the doctrine of the essential corruption of man.

Such a doctrine had many repercussions. It made salvation a matter of grace alone. The natural man, in contrast to the regenerate man, cannot do anything of his own toward salvation, because his mind is too darkened, his will too weakened by original sin. This explains the Lutheran position that grace, rather than good works, is essential to salvation. Man, as natural man, could not do good works; only through grace could good works be done. So grace is the essential thing, and good works are the coincidental expression of grace. Milton reflects this doctrine in a speech of the Archangel Michael in *Paradise Lost* (XII, 285 ff.), in which he mentions man's "natural pravity":

> To whom thus Michael. Doubt not but that sin
> Will reign among them, as of thee begot;
> And therefore was Law given them to evince
> Thir natural pravity, by stirring up
> Sin against Law to fight; that when they see
> Law can discover sin, but not remove,
> Save by those shadowy expiations weak,
> The blood of Bulls and Goats, they may conclude

The Historical Genesis

> Some blood more precious must be paid for Man,
> Just for unjust, that in such righteousness
> To them by Faith imputed, they may find
> Justification towards God, and peace
> Of Conscience, which the Law by Ceremonies
> Cannot appease, nor Man the moral part
> Perform, and not performing cannot live.

Michael here speaks as a straightforward Calvinist. Salvation is through "imputed righteousness." This latter term implies that the essential nature of man is what it is (corrupt) but can be covered and made presentable to the Creator by righteousness being bestowed on man from an outside source. Milton has this in mind when he speaks symbolically of nature hiding her guilty front with innocent snow in "On the Morning of Christ's Nativity" (line 40). In commenting on Christ's action in clothing the nakedness of Adam and Eve, Milton is even more explicit about this doctrine:

> Nor hee thir outward only with the Skins
> Of Beasts, but inward nakedness, much more
> Opprobrious, with his Robe of righteousness,
> Arraying cover'd from his Father's sight.
> (Paradise Lost X, 220–223)

The problem naturally arises that, if man cannot make sound moral decisions ("nor Man the moral part/Perform") antecedent to the bestowal of grace, on what basis is grace actually given? The answer in Calvinism is that grace is bestowed arbitrarily. The Thomistic position had been more complicated, because it had presumed that man could accept or reject grace at his discretion—that man *of himself* did a good work in accepting grace. The arbitrary bestowal of grace leads inevitably to a clear-cut doctrine of predestination.

Milton rebels against this doctrine, as many Puritan preachers did. In this matter he is a follower of the theologian Arminius (1560–1609), who, while reluctant to split entirely with the Calvinist position, modifies it in the direction of free will. In *Paradise Lost* God himself speaks on behalf of free will as against predestination:

> ... They therefore as to right belong'd,
> So were created, nor can justly accuse
> Thir maker, or thir making, or thir Fate;
> As if Predestination over-rul'd
> Thir will, dispos'd by absolute Decree
> Or high foreknowledge; they themselves decreed
> Thir own revolt, not I; if I foreknew,
> Foreknowledge had no influence on their fault,
> Which had no less prov'd certain unforeknown.
> (III, 111–119)

While some are predestined to salvation or damnation, Milton, along with Arminius, presumes the existence of another third class who may or may not respond to grace. Again in *Paradise Lost* God the Father says:

> The rest shall hear me call, and oft be warn'd
> Thir sinful state, and to appease betimes
> Th' incensed Deity while offer'd grace
> Invites. ... (III, 185–188)

A novice to Milton, but otherwise informed on the history of ideas, might reasonably expect that Milton, following Late Augustinian tradition, would take a dim view of "natural" man and of "natural" reason, for this would be in keeping with the specific attitudes of Luther and of Calvin.[5]

Milton's position (while not always consistent—God the Father in the epic makes most of Milton's Calvinist pronouncements) is nearer to medievalism than to Calvinism in these matters. Milton says that the word *nature* means "either the essence of a thing, or that general law which is the origin of every thing and under which every thing acts."[6] As far as "essence" being corrupted, Milton states in *De Doctrina Christiana*: "There can be no doubt that for the purpose of vindicating the justice of God, especially in his calling of mankind, it is much better to allow to man (whether as a remnant of his primitive state, or as restored through the operation of grace whereby he is called) some portion of free will in respect of good works, or at least of good endeavors. . . . For if our personal religion were not in some degree dependent on ourselves, and in our own power, God could not properly enter into a covenant with us; neither could we perform, much less swear to perform, the conditions of that covenant."[7] This is very close to the position that Maurice de Wulf attributes to the medieval Scholastics: "They did not believe that the Fall of Adam had caused the complete corruption of man, or of nature in general. Free will, they almost all agreed, remained whole; and even that true liberty, 'the will to do right,' which most of them distinguished from morally indifferent choice, had been restored through the efficacy of grace. Man had been mutilated perhaps, but 'nothing can efface from conscience the fundamental tendency toward goodness. . . .' "[8]

Though Milton rejects the exclusive Calvinist emphasis on grace, he does not observe as closely as his medieval predecessors the distinction between the order of reason and the order of grace. Such a distinction underlies the structure of Dante's epic; Virgil symbolizes reason and Beatrice, grace. The virtues of reason—prudence, justice, fortitude, and temperance—were considered as attainable by all men even when the Christian faith (in the sense of supernatural knowledge) had not illuminated their lives. Edmund Spenser had tried courageously, but not altogether convincingly, to observe the two orders, with a view toward an ultimate synthesis. Spenser's Holiness, Chastity, Courtesy had specifically Christian references which Aristotle, in his system of the virtues, had not anticipated; their Greek sense was at least unconsciously changed due to a long Christian tradition. The Aristotelian concept of virtue as a mean between excess and deficiency could not always square with a concept like that of charity—surely, as described in the words of St. Paul, an excess (bearing all things, believing all things, hoping all things, enduring all things). In *The Faerie Queene*, Charissa (charity) in the House of Holiness and Una (divine grace) present the deepest medieval values but are removed from Aristotle by a whole body of Christian doctrine. Spenser attempted some sort of compromise with the more secular humanism of the Renaissance by making Magnificence and Glory the unitive virtues, rather than Holiness, in so far as the total structure of *The Faerie Queene* is concerned. But even Glory is a Christianized virtue, having overtones of medieval sanctification. Sir Thomas More had to observe the distinction between nature and grace in the *Utopia* closely, because this distinction was essential to his satiric message: that the Utopians living a life of reason were doing a better job than Europeans to whom the benefits of revelation and divine grace had been offered.

Like More, Milton would have argued that "Reason is servant to Faith, not enemy,"[9] but, in the tradition of radical Protestantism and in contrast to much medieval thinking, Milton enlarges the area of grace. In common with Protestant tradition, he has an unrestricted optimism about knowledge as Late Augustinian illumination, about knowledge as a correlative of piety—infused knowledge from the Holy Spirit:

> God hath now sent his living Oracle
> Into the World to teach his final will,

The Historical Genesis

And sends his Spirit of Truth henceforth to dwell
In pious Hearts, an inward Oracle
To all truth requisite for men to know.
(*Paradise Regained* I, 460–464)

RADICAL PROTESTANTISM VERSUS THE CHURCH OF ENGLAND

It would be misleading to think that fine points of theology were a main concern of people at the time of the Reformation, in spite of its being a religiously orientated age. It is not an exaggeration to say that popular support for the Protestant movement on the Continent was in great measure due to what we are accustomed to call "social protest." Many serious-minded people were disenchanted with the way affairs were being administered by the central authorities in Rome. While it is easy to speak, in a blanket phrase, of the corruption of the church, the ticklish situation underlying "corruption" had long historical roots. A main problem was the fact that church and state were intertwined in an uneasy relationship, and the church dignitary was often a medieval baron. Many of the popes seemed to be much more concerned with the politics of the Papal States than they were with the meaning and destiny of the universal church. An outstanding example and, of course, a somewhat eccentric one is the Borgia family. Machiavelli particularly admired Caesar Borgia, Pope Alexander's son, because of the decisive, brilliant, and unscrupulous way in which he was extending papal political power. He saw in Caesar Borgia the prototype of the future leader who was to bring about a united Italy.

Medieval churchmen were also fighting soldiers. In Sir Thomas More's time English bishops and abbots fought in wars against Scotland and at Flodden Field (1513) may have cleaved Scottish skulls with their own battle-axes.[10] This was not, of course, in their capacity as good shepherds but in that of medieval barons. Pope Julius II, the patron of Michelangelo, an old man who was frequently on the point of dying and then of suddenly recovering vigorous health, arose from a sick bed to lead an attack on an Italian castle and personally breach its walls.[11]

The confused relationship of church and state throughout the Middle Ages ultimately brought the church into a nearly impossible moral quandary. As a consequence, the impact of the Protestant revolution was at least as social and political as theological. In the case of Luther, the Pope paid very little attention to him when the young man first came to his notice. He assumed that Luther's problems were the traditional ones of theological controversies on extremely difficult subject matters (in line with medieval academic traditions of the debate) and dismissed the subject as another quarrel among the monks. But when Martin Luther preached against the collection of Peter's pence, here was a practical and financial matter that could not be ignored. The break in Christian unity, while a most extensive thing and very possibly a tragic thing, originated in a number of restricted and even trivial crises, the import of which no one seemed clearly to recognize at first.

When we come to consider England itself, we have a very different situation from that which prevailed on the Continent. The Reformation on the Continent might be described as a grass-roots affair with a large measure of popular support. In England, the Reformation came from above. Henry VIII was in the medieval tradition of a leader of a national state who wished to extend his supposed authority against the central administration of the church. This had been a long medieval feud. Many times the Holy Roman Emperor wished to regard the church as the spiritual arm of the state. On the other hand, some popes were theocrats and wished to regard the state as the secular arm

The Historical Genesis

of the church. We witness Henry IV standing for hours in the snow before the Castle of Canossa, begging for an interview with Hildebrand. On the other hand, in the fourteenth century we have the Babylonian captivity at Avignon, where the popes were, for all practical purposes, the political prisoners of the French kings. This church-state relationship seesawed back and forth with no clear line of guiding principles; Dante in the *Divine Comedy* gives a graphic symbolism to this turmoil.

Henry VIII started his effort to obtain political jurisdiction over the church in England by rather mild measures, such as an act of praemunire forbidding appeals from English ecclesiastical courts to Rome. This did not seriously disturb anyone. In fact, an English bishop who had made a judgment in an ecclesiastical trial could conceivably have felt pleased that his own decision would be regarded as final and there would be no repercussions through an appeal to Rome. The problem became more accentuated, of course, when Henry VIII demanded an Oath of Supremacy from officeholders, in effect recognizing Henry as head of the church in England. The bishops met in solemn convocation and, with one exception, that of Cardinal Fisher who was convicted of high treason and beheaded (1535) as a warning to the others, they agreed to such acknowledgment but with an important reservation. They acknowledged (1531) Henry as head of the church in England, *as far as the law of God allowed*.[12] The meaning of this reservation was not spelled out, and obviously it was a compromise which avoided pressing the issue to a final conflict. This decision proved later to have been cautious rather than prudent and, in the end, disastrous from the bishops' point of view, because eight years after the convocation met there was not a house of religion left in England.[13]

The attitude of Henry VIII theologically was that of an extreme conservative. He maintained the main body of Catholic

11

doctrine with scarcely any disturbance at all, except in the question of final authority. A peculiar irony attaches to all that Henry VIII did. Upon him was conferred the highest Catholic distinction ever bestowed on a layman in the history of the church. He was entitled "Defender of the Faith," because he wrote the *Assertion of the Seven Sacraments* in reply to Luther's *Babylonish Captivity of the Church*. In *The Life of Sir Thomas More* by William Roper, More's son-in-law, we are informed that More did not share Henry's extravagant support of the papacy. In fact, he warned the King of possible future conflict with the Pope in the latter's capacity as a temporal prince. "I said unto his Grace, I must put your Grace in remembrance of one thing, and that is this, the Pope (as your Grace knoweth) is a Prince as you are, and in league with all other Christian Princes, that may hereafter so fall out, that your Grace and he may vary on some points of the league, whereupon may grow some breach of amity and war between you both; I think it best therefore that that place be amended, and his authority more slenderly touched."[14] Sir Thomas More was, by his own life and death, instrumental in helping to clarify to some extent this confused relationship between church and state.

The position which the Roman Church ultimately adopted, that the state is supreme in its own sphere but that on certain ultimate matters of faith and conscience the church holds precedence, was the result of many generations of bitter experience and extensive thinking. The relationship of church to state in the time of Henry VIII—and, of course, through the later Church of England-Puritan conflicts—was in a state of flux and agitation. Henry's impact on religion was that of a prime mover, and the handling of religion became a matter of Tudor national policy.

As we have said, we did not witness in England a popular religious revolution as we did on the Continent. Henry VIII left three children by three different wives, and each of them, in succeeding in turn to the throne, took up a different position in regard to religion. Edward VI reigned only briefly, and he seems to have fallen under the advice of those leaning toward radical Protestantism, for some effort was made to guide the Church of England in the direction of Continental Protestantism. This tendency was reversed by his half-sister Mary, who made the serious political mistake of trying to restore Roman Catholicism by direct pressure and alienated her people. In the time of Elizabeth, the policy of her father, Henry VIII, was restored. Elizabeth wanted a church that made for stability and that was in harmony with the political direction of the crown. Laws were passed against both recusants and dissenters, and were enforced or not enforced according to the persons and political contexts involved.

But Elizabethan controls were mainly political and did not touch the emotional depths of the country. We see sown, almost unconsciously, the seeds of the religious civil war that was to follow in the seventeenth century. The Established Church with its still existent Catholic tradition and those Protestants who had become more and more convinced of the position of radical Protestantism would not be able to compromise.[15] While Roman Catholicism ceased to have any important influence on English affairs, England could by no means be considered a *unified* Protestant country. The religious differences ran deep (to which could be added economic and social differences, but this was a period in which religion was even more important than these), and in Milton's time we witness the climax to this state of affairs.

MILTON AND RADICAL PROTESTANTISM

Three major groups constituted radical Protestantism in England. Though Presbyterianism was deeply rooted in Scotland, its influence was also felt in England. An interesting aspect of the development of Presbyterianism and other groups outside the Church of England was the continued antipathy toward the organizational forms of the Roman Church and even toward their memory. The same bitterness was directed against the survival of such forms in the Anglican Church. The word *bishop* became a repulsive word for many Protestants. Yet the church of John Knox in Scotland and the home church in Geneva had a very powerful ecclesiastical organization, though such clergy were known as *presbyters* rather than as bishops. Milton was led to say, after he had become disenchanted with Presbyterianism, that the "new Presbyter is but old priest writ large."[16] The Presbyterians constituted a highly self-disciplined body, and, although we are placing them under the label of radical Protestants, in another sense and especially in contrast with what we call the Independents, they can be considered quite conservative, relying on a highly organized social-religious structure. In their struggle with Charles I they were comparatively moderate and diplomatic, wishing in the main to assure their own autonomy and rights.

The Congregationalists had their inception in England. The theory underlying the Congregational churches was that each congregation was a self-sufficient unit corresponding through prayer with God directly. Various churches should have sisterly relations with one another, but the Congregational theology was opposed to any central organization. Both Presbyterians and Congregationalists found reason for their particular attitudes in one analysis or another of the attitudes and behavior of the early church, based on scriptural passages. The Congregationalists, in addition to the Presbyterians, might be considered to belong to the conservative side of radical Protestantism.

The Historical Genesis

It was the third group, the Independents, who constituted religious radicalism in every sense. They were radical in the sense of being revolutionary politically and economically, as well as in the meaning of going back to the *radices* or roots of scriptural tradition, as in the case of the groups above. Their revolutionary aspect, their idol-smashing, appealed to a strong revolutionary temperament in Milton himself. In the Independency we have the ultimate result of one Protestant point of view—that if an individual reads the Bible in a spirit of sincerity, and without the necessity of any other guidance, the Holy Spirit will give him sufficient understanding and grace to interpret the Bible justly and rightly, at least in a measure sufficient to assure his salvation. A large number of overt statements indicates that the scholarly Milton himself held this view. Some rather fantastic notions derived from highly individualistic interpretations of the Scriptures, including the temporarily influential views of the Fifth Monarchy men. Milton at one time shared some of their milennial views (see Chapter II). Some movements, even more to the left than the Independency, were much more influential than others and had in them the potentiality of severe cultural and economic revolution. This was particularly true in regard to the Levellers. They had the idea, always inflammatory, of sharing the wealth, of economic egalitarianism, a point of view always enthusiastically supported by the underprivileged and viewed with corresponding distaste by property owners. By 1649 Cromwell was proposing to punish and exile Levellers. Actually the most revolutionary aim that the Independents succeeded in accomplishing was the execution of Charles I, with which Milton was in entire sympathy as he so often restates in *A Defence of the People of England* (1651).

How does Milton fit into the course of these events? Milton is certainly no detached observer of the current scenes. He tells us in *A Second Defence of the English People* (1654) why he interrupted his European tour: "Although I desired also to cross to Sicily and Greece, the sad tidings of civil war from England summoned me back. For I thought it base that I should travel abroad at my ease for the cultivation of my mind, while my fellow-citizens at home were fighting for their liberty."[17] After writing a series of works (*Of Reformation in England,* 1641; *Animadversions,* 1641; *The Reason of Church Government,* 1642; *An Apology Against a Modest Confutation,* 1642) and "after the bishops, at whom every man aimed his arrow, had at length fallen," Milton began to turn his thoughts to other subjects. He began to consider "whether I could in any way advance the cause of true and substantial liberty, which must be sought, not without, but within, and which is best achieved, not by the sword, but by a life rightly undertaken and rightly conducted."[18]

Milton had attended Christ College, Cambridge, where there seemed to exist a definite, though unorganized encouragement for outstanding graduates to enter the ministry of the Church of England with a view to reforming it from within and bringing it to a more radical Protestant position. Rather than following the road of the dissenters, with all the possible disadvantages of legal persecution, suitable young men by climbing the ecclesiastical ladder and working from within could exercise a constructive long-term influence on the Anglican Church. The hero of "Lycidas" was such a candidate. But it is significant that, in the poem, while Milton praises the prospective minister Edward King, he damns the hierarchy. The attack on the Church of England, voiced with indignation and acerbic brilliance, had specific poetic precedents in Spenser's *The Shepheardes Calender,* for there had been a long history of such dissatisfaction. Milton felt too keenly about the situation in the Established Church to follow the pattern of compromise set by the admired Edward

The Historical Genesis

King. Milton makes his position absolutely clear in *The Reason of Church Government*: "The Church, to whose service by the intentions of my parents and friends I was destined of a child, and in mine own resolutions, till coming to some maturity of years and perceiving what tyranny had invaded the church, that he who would take orders must subscribe slave and take an oath withal, which, unless he took it with a conscience that would retch, he must either straight perjure or split his faith; I thought it better to prefer a blameless silence before the sacred office of speaking, bought and begun with servitude and forswearing."[19]

In entering the public marketplace of religious and political controversy (for politics and religion were closely allied in his time), Milton is a somewhat ironic figure, for it can be plausibly argued that he is the last great man of the Renaissance. He has a largeness, an exuberance, a versatility, a sense of grandeur and of glory that seem inappropriate to sectarian controversy. His work is a synthesis of many traditions (even when he insists upon being untraditional) and exhibits a vast erudition. He is a versatile synthesizer of the type made famous in the Renaissance. He is a poet (lyric, epic, dramatic), a political philosopher, a theologian. Fundamentally he has the uninhibited confidence of the Renaissance man in carrying out vast intricate designs, to which the acquiring of universal knowledge seems to be merely a preliminary step. Milton never doubted that the proper education could produce men of his own type. "I call therefore a complete and generous education that which fits a man to perform justly, skilfully, and magnanimously all the offices both private and public of peace and war."[20]

Milton sees himself as the classical man of letters who also leads a magnanimous life of civic action. Though primarily a thinker, he is also the public man who will offer guiding principles on the larger issues. He thinks, in the *Areopagitica* (1644), of the greatness of a nation and of the acquiring of knowledge as correlatives. In the eloquent terms of the classical orator, Milton sees "a noble and puissant nation rousing herself like a strong man after sleep, and shaking her invincible locks. Methinks I see her as an eagle muing [moulting] her mighty youth, and kindling her undazzled eyes at the full midday beam...." Why, he asks, should anyone "suppress all this flowery crop of knowledge and new light sprung up"?[21]

However studiously he tackles a subject, however many the authorities he cites and the allusions he makes, almost instinctively Milton assumes the mantle of a Demosthenes, a Cicero. Inspired partly by his classical reading, he was very conscious of the civic spirit and the proud meaning of the word *citizen* —the public-spirited, self-reliant citizen who is opposed to tyrannies of all kinds. The concept of the citizen in Milton is really much nearer to the Roman model than to that of the Puritan elect, the "enthusiast," which motivated many of his contemporaries.

Milton's participation in public life follows an idealist pattern reminiscent of the philosopher-king in Plato's *Republic*. He is not a politician deeply concerned with the art of the possible but, rather, a teacher, a keeper of the nation's conscience.

Because he moves in an age of the religious enthusiasts, Milton's idealistic public role is historically more plausible. Nevertheless, within the context of political causes a poet may look very much like anyone else in public life—except that the poet, laying aside the tremendous powers that are peculiarly his, may appear diminished and even at times a trifle absurd. Any political ineptitudes, shaky generalizations, or petulances on his part loom larger and more grotesque than they would in a lesser man, especially if he is drawn into partisan political debate, as Milton was.

The Historical Genesis

Fortunately Milton expressed the narrower aspects of his personality in prose rather than in poetry. If conviction, affirmation, reverence, fervor are to enter into a work of poetry, the didactic and the polemical must be transcended. Prose does not have to go beyond a level amenable to a solid but routine system of judgment. In prose we are not usually confronted with something beyond our ordinary intellectual capacity, with the mysterious allusiveness of metaphoric structure, or insights which we cannot alertly and immediately comprehend.

Milton is a polemicist as well as a poet, and in this role he may seem to have too much energy and "singularity" for modern taste. We are just not accustomed to seeing so much productivity by one man in various fields which today would be assigned to specialists. Moreover, Milton exhibits a wide range of individualistic views. While the reader may feel sympathetic to one or several of them, the package is so large that it may cause a reader to suspect Milton's judgment.

Research has shown there was a considerable measure of support for all of Milton's special views and a background of tradition had been established for them among the sects and controversies of sixteenth- and seventeenth-century Protestantism. But Milton has the disadvantage of being involved in several controversies that were to become lost in history. The issue of prelacy in his day was a hot and tormenting one, touching upon many sensitivities, but today, even after we have identified the various participants and the ramifications of their views, we still have difficulty in seeing such a matter come alive.

It is useful, however, to take note of the principal ideas expressed in the narrower partisan context of Milton's prose as well as in the more universal one of his poetry. The same basic range of ideas is covered in both poetry and prose, though the effects are very different. Especially, the treatise *De Doctrina Christiana*, a massive nonpolitical (and, comparatively speaking, nonpolemical) theological work, affords many important keys to interpreting Milton's *Paradise Lost* as well as to the general development of his thought.

MILTON'S CONCEPT OF FREEDOM

A central body of Milton's thought clusters around the concept of freedom. If this concept is entered into in depth, practically every theological and philosophical crux might have to be considered as well. Anyone who has attempted merely to define the elements that enter into the idea of freedom becomes aware of how static and relatively immobile conceptual language is. Unless used with the greatest skill, it tends to make ideas stand out like great monoliths, great rocks of Gibralter, which are inadequate symbols for fluidity, creativity, and evolutionary aspects of reality. The eighteenth-century poetic habit of capitalizing ("personifying") abstractions is an unconscious confession of the frustration we all experience in the verbal effort to realize the complexity of reality. In order to attain some sort of precision, the scientist has long abandoned any system of ordinary words, but the philosopher and the theologian are still dependent upon them. Words remain essential to the poet, who is able to employ constructively their intuitive suggestiveness and is better able to suggest the fluidity of reality than an intellectual dealing with ideas through an imprecise language. Milton, however, is a philosopher and theologian as well as a poet, and we shall have several occasions to point out how the context of a work of art alters appreciably what Milton wants to convey intellectually.

Milton also runs into the same danger we perceive today, that theological language seems to many rather outworn and unadjusted to the increasing discoveries of modern science, psychology, physics. The complex emotional content, for example, traditionally evoked by the word *God* cannot any longer be relied upon. We may have a wide range of different associations (and most of them involve further problems)—the Freudian "father-image," the relationship of being and existence, relativity, new concepts of time and space, and so on.

Theological tradition did not offer much help in defining the tensions of the word *"freedom"* in Milton's time. An important distinction was assumed (as in *Paradise Lost*) between the earthly freedom of man's condition and the heavenly freedom of man's beatitude. Something we associate with earthly freedom—the possibility that choices may be made that go seriously and tragically wrong—is removed from the elect who have found sanctification and glorification. Their freedom is jelled in attitudes of rectitude. It is assumed that the saved have some built-in guarantee against the abuse of their freedom, a guarantee not extended to the fallen angels and to Adam. Such a concept of freedom involves quite different definitions than the concept of freedom that is related to our own direct experience, and to which we refer in such heart-easing terms as "calculated risk," and "worthwhile gamble," when we speak of the tremendous values that somehow must arise from hazardous crises. The dignity of man has been associated repeatedly with that perilous freedom that he may exercise well—or badly.

In effect, Milton presents in his major masterpiece, *Paradise Lost*, the earthly freedom rather than the heavenly one. Whatever the dangers of the earthly freedom, it makes for suspense and excitement in a work of art.

Any presentation of the human freedom in relation to a Creator must present the latter as a gambler. The great stories of Job, Faust, and of Milton's Satan symbolize a bizarre but basically logical situation: Once granted free choice man can be the subject of cosmic bets. Fortunately, in the cases of both Job and Faust, Providence won in the end but not without great uncertainty and tension. To some extent radical Protestantism loses the sense of the existential gambler, the man who is hovering amid such paradoxes as the last shall be first and the one who loses his life shall save it. Milton had some sense of the narrowness of view implicit in the doctrine of election and predestination. He expresses it in those mysterious and paradoxical lines that relate salvation to the renouncing of righteous as well as unrighteous deeds (*Paradise Lost* III, 292). God the Father is rather Calvinistic (as we shall explain in Chapter III), but there is no doubt about the presentation of Adam as an existential gambler in his use of freedom.

In his concept of freedom, Milton, in keeping with the radical Protestant tradition of an all-embracing sin and an all-embracing conversion and election, does not envisage any series of falls and recoveries as is accepted, for example, by the Roman Church. The possibility that Adam might subsequently sin as seriously as he did in the instance of the forbidden fruit does not concern Milton. He follows St. Augustine, who in *The City of God* (XXII, xxii) maintained that all Adam's children were condemned in him.[22] In *De Doctrina Christiana* Milton maintains that the Fall included all sins: "For what sin can be named, which was not included in this one act? It comprehended at once distrust in the divine veracity, and a proportionate credulity in the assurances of Satan; unbelief; ingratitude; disobedience; gluttony; in the man excessive uxoriousness, in the woman a want of proper regard for her husband, in both an insensibility to the welfare of their offspring, and that offspring the whole human race. . . ."[23]

Theologically speaking, the loss of freedom was for Milton final in original sin. It could be recovered by a regeneration that would also be final—but on new and different terms from those prior to the Fall. Northrop Frye once stated that "in a Catholic poet—Dante is the obvious example—the separation of the divine and demonic worlds would be something that man sees or participates in through a process of sacramental discipline, which continues in the next world in the form of purgatory. But for Milton such revelation cannot come from anything continuous, however important habit and discipline may be in themselves. The place of sacrament and purgatory in his work is taken by the temptation, the agon or contest which is the theme of all four of his major poems."[24] Milton insistently repeats that the assurance of virtue can only be obtained by trial. However, he seems to incorporate all trials in one trial just as he incorporates all sins in original sin. In the *Reason of Church Government* I, vii, he states, "for if there were no opposition, where were the trial of an unfeigned goodness and magnanimity? Virtue that wavers is not virtue, but vice revolted from itself and after a while returning."[25] Milton never quite clarifies the question: When is a man wise, before or after temptation? Does the surmounting of temptation simply demonstrate that a man already possessed wisdom? Or does the temptation itself produce a growth in wisdom—the man becomes wise through resisting temptation? The latter situation seems true of Adam and Samson: the former of the Lady in *Comus* and of Christ in *Paradise Regained*.

POLITICAL FREEDOM AND NATURAL HIERARCHY

Society has to go on, even if the individual is faced with heroic temptation. The morning paper and the milk must be delivered and taxes have to be paid, even while man is suspended between heaven and hell. Someone has to govern while others have to be governed, and occasionally individuals, like Charles I, are executed.

The basic Miltonic thesis is that tyrants impose upon freedom and win the right to be destroyed. In his concept of political freedom, Milton constantly refers to the law of nature. His final justification for the execution of Charles I was that primary and general law of nature, which according to the will of God (and, therefore, to right reason) holds that whatever is for the safety of the state is just and right.[26] Unfortunately the people (in a collective sense) seldom know what the people's good is. Milton had to justify a spiritual élite (in his *A Defence of the People of England*), a minority but the highest embodiment of the people's will, in their taking control of England without regard for the ordinary legal procedures. When it is alleged that the form of government which has been set up in England is not a people's government but that of the military, Milton does not see any real problem. "I say it was the people; for why should I not say that the act of the better, the sound part of the Parliament, in which resides the real power of the people, was the act of the people? If a majority in Parliament prefer enslavement and putting the commonwealth up for sale, is it not right for a minority to prevent it if they can and preserve their freedom?"[27]

Milton obviously solves the dilemma sometimes faced by the democratic liberal, in his support of freedom, in a rather doctrinaire way. The people should freely decide as long as they decide right. But what if they decide wrong? In that event an enlightened minority must take over and decide for them—for their better future selves, so to speak. This is analogous to the democratic process as Karl Marx understood it. This point of view is a gentle and ironic reminder to those of us who may fall and recover many times, who lack the absolute assurance that we possess right reason, of the dangers that may be run at the hands

The Historical Genesis

of idealistic reformers no less than at the hands of practical men grinding away at politics, the necessary but grubby art of the possible.

When pressed by his opponent Salmasius, Milton attempts to meet the thorny problem of legal precedent in the execution of Charles I by recourse to the law of nature. "If you still demand 'By what right or what law?,' my reply is 'By that law of Nature and of God. . . .'"[28] In the *De Doctrina Christiana* Milton observes that the law of nature is "implanted and innate" and is sufficient of itself "to teach whatever is agreeable to right reason, that is to say, whatever is intrinsically good."[29] In terms of these simple identifications, the execution of Charles I was in accord with right reason and intrinsically good.

Among Milton's applications of the law of nature was that a free people is not bound by the statute of any preceding parliaments but by the law of nature only, "which is the only law of laws truly and properly fundamental to all mankind."[30] It is in accordance with the law of nature that what is superior by nature should rule what is inferior, even if it is necessary to use force. "Certainly by the law of nature all good kings always consider the Senate or people as their equal and their superior. Since however a tyrant is by nature the lowest of all men, whoever has more power than he must be considered his equal and superior. Just as once under nature's guidance men advanced from the use of force to laws, so of necessity they must follow the same guide and return to force when laws are disregarded."[31] Milton is speaking here in terms of broad theory. He does not envisage any juridical procedure by which it can be determined who is superior by nature. The making of decisions—even wrong ones by the wrong person for the wrong reasons—might conceivably be preferable at times, in the practical order, to the possibility of general slaughter brought about by tests of strength.

Milton is concerned with the kind of authority exercised by magistrates as well as by kings. Milton considers the king only as a special kind of magistrate. The power of kings and magistrates "is nothing else, but what is only derivative, transferred and committed to them in trust from the people to the common good of them all, in whom the power yet remains fundamentally, and cannot be taken from them without a violation of their natural birthright."[32] The question would seem to be purely academic, whether the regenerate, following a higher law of nature, would necessarily be subject to a magistrate, since their relationship to him would be one of convenience rather than of necessity. They would not be subject to the unjust decisions of a magistrate any more than to those of Charles I. The function of a magistrate among the elect would be that of arbitration rather than judgment.

It is not easy to clarify the role of freedom in Milton's political philosophy, partially because he uses the word *people* sometimes in a general sense but often with the connotation of "the better part." Strictly speaking, according to the Calvinists, the only man who is truly free is the man who belongs to the elect, but it was impossible to define such a group within the political order. Even in Milton there is a certain amount of confusion between freedom in the sense of the freedom of the sons of God —the freedom of the true believer who has gone through the cycle of election, justification, and sanctification—and freedom in a nonreligious, specifically political sense.

Arthur Barker has pointed out that Milton thinks of a primary and a secondary law of nature.[33] "Prime nature"—nature before the Fall—"has made us all equal, made us equal coheirs by common right and dominion over all creatures."[34] But because of the subsequent decay from original righteousness, nature "suffered not only divorce but all that which by civilians is termed 'the secondary law of nature and of nations.' "[35] The secondary law of nature is an imperfect expression of the original law of nature. Under the gospel, however, there is a "second fresh penciling of the eternal law by the spirit in the hearts of the believers, a renewal of the law originally engraven in Adam's breast." The law of nature, therefore, sometimes refers to the law as it would apply to the regenerate as in a Christian commonwealth. In this sense, it is only the regenerate who are capable of the *natural* liberty which is the end of just government. But, in a secondary sense, the law of nature may also apply to the natural right of any people, Christian or otherwise, to freedom from tyranny, but not necessarily to the right of natural liberty, a very different matter.

Milton did not see in institutions a guarantee and perpetuation of freedom; rather they were threats to it. He does not see the state as necessary and natural to man even in an unfallen condition. Church and state were, at best, necessary evils due to unregeneracy among mankind.

Puritanism was confused between the heavenly freedom and the earthly freedom. The elect were trying to enjoy a heavenly freedom in an earthly environment. In its optimism that institutions were unnecessary (Milton never thought of putting a church in Paradise), Puritanism was self-defeating in the political order. It affords an example, rare in history, of a revolution which was successful through its early fervor but which eventually simply faded away. It was not overthrown, or even seriously threatened, by a counterrevolution. Not psychologically attuned to institutions, it did not set up strong institutions to perpetuate itself.

Milton, as a highly gifted man, intellectually and imaginatively, had a built-in resistance against domination by mediocrity, political or ecclesiastical. In temperament a classical aristocrat, he viewed the multitude with extreme reserve. He was a Platonist, not a practical politician, and James Harrington's statement in *The Commonwealth of Oceana* (1656)—so obvious because so true—that "the wisdom of the few may be the light of mankind; but the interest of the few is not the profit of mankind nor of a commonwealth"[36] would not have appealed to this supporter of élite reformers.

In so far as the heavenly freedom is presented in *Paradise Lost*, Milton avoids certain tensions in the idea of freedom, because God, as the absolute, is there to put everything right. He is all that all institutions could be at their best in one. Thus, in the heavenly freedom there is no problem about the principle of natural hierarchy, that what is superior by nature should govern what is lower, because heaven is presided over by an intelligence who views all things at one view. At best, the earthly city could set up only very imperfect norms for a natural hierarchy, because imperfect men judge imperfect men. Milton has no tensions about kings and magistrates in the heavenly freedom, which, interestingly enough, is symbolized by a king. In Book VI of *Paradise Lost* Abdiel argues, like an orthodox conservative, that freedom lies in the implementation of the commands of rightful authority, which among angels is expressed without intermediaries in a God-to-person theocracy. To attempt to evade this rightful authority is to create a new kind of tyranny, that of the self, which replaces a true objective order:

> Unjustly thou deprav'st it with the name
> Of *Servitude* to serve whom God ordains,
> Or Nature; God and Nature bid the same,
> When he who rules is worthiest, and excels
> Them whom he governs. This is servitude,
> To serve th' unwise, or him who hath rebell'd

Against his worthier, as thine now serve thee,
Thyself not free, but to thyself enthrall'd....
(*Paradise Lost* VI, 174–181)

The great advantage of the heavenly freedom is that hierarchy is a state of facts. In the earthly city, natural hierarchy is a matter of surmise, and functions have to be carried on by people who just happen to hold the offices.

NOTES

[1] St. Augustine, *The City of God*, trans. John Healey (Edinburgh, 1909) II, 2.

[2] *Ibid.*, 24.

[3] *Ibid.*, 358.

[4] "There is, nevertheless, an irreconcilable cleavage between the attitude of Luther and that of St. Augustine. Nowhere in the writings of the Bishop of Hippo will be found the radical condemnation of human nature which constantly flows from the pen of Luther. Quite on the contrary, fallen nature remains in his eyes so beautiful, so good, and so great, that he did not hesitate to say that had God created it such as it is after the Fall, it would still suffice to prove the infinite wisdom of its author. This theme, which I have elsewhere proposed to call the 'eulogy of fallen nature' seems to me to express admirably the essential aspects of authentic Augustinianism, that, namely of St. Augustine himself." Etienne Gilson, *Christianity and Philosophy* (London and New York, 1939) 9–10.

[5] For a modern position that follows identically the original Calvinist tradition see Jacques Ellul, "Concerning the Christian Attitude Towards Law," *The Christian Scholar* XLII, No. 2 (June, 1959) 139–150. "The doctrine of the natural law is one aspect of the heresy which affirms a harmony between Grace and Nature" (144). "We should perhaps recall that the theory of the natural law is not at all Christian in spite of a quasi unanimity among theologians since St. Augustine which has misled the Church in this direction. Biblically, no textual agreement allows us to speak of natural law. Only Romans 2:14 may allow us perhaps to see some allusion to it, without however giving us any precise details. [Romans

2:14 reads: "When the Gentiles who have no law do by nature what the Law prescribes, those having no law are a law unto themselves."] All the conception of law in the Old Testament is opposed to this idea" (143). Ellul's views are ultimately based on the original rigorous Calvinist interpretation of original sin: "In the situation created by the Fall, the world is at the same time the totality of powers which are in rebellion to God and all that radically sinful man can create and invent. Just as no man is exempt from sin, so nothing that he is able to invent is beyond the realm of sin. The World belongs to the Prince of this World —it is not because the world is good or merited it but precisely because the world is lost, rebellious, and evil" (139). If justice were inscribed in man's nature as such, the Calvinist doctrine of justification by faith would be eliminated (143). It is easy to see how Milton's views differ materially from strict Calvinism.

[6] *The Christian Doctrine* I, ii, *The Works of John Milton*, ed. Frank Allen Patterson (New York: Columbia University Press, 1931–1938) 18 vols in 21—hereafter referred to as CE—XIV, 27.

[7] *The Christian Doctrine* I, xii, CE, XV, 213–215.

[8] Maurice de Wulf, *Philosophy and Civilization in the Middle Ages* (London and Princeton, N. J., 1922) 137.

[9] *The Utopia of Sir Thomas More*, ed. J. H. Lupton (Oxford, 1895) 190.

[10] Cf. Russell Ames, *Citizen Thomas More and His Utopia* (Princeton, 1949) 149.

[11] Ralph Roeder, *Man of the Renaissance* (New York, 1933) 260.

[12] R. W. Chambers, *Thomas More* (New York, 1935) 248.

[13] *Ibid.*, 358.

[14] William Roper, *The Life of Sir Thomas More* (New York: Everyman Library, 1925) 46.

[15] Cf. Milton's observation: "Henry VIII was the first that rent this kingdom from the pope's subjection totally; but his quarrel being more about supremacy, than other faultiness in religion that he regarded, it is no marvel that he stuck where he did. The next default was in the bishops, who, though they had renounced the pope, they still hugged the popedom, and shared the authority among themselves, by their six bloody articles, persecuting the protestants no slacker than the pope would have done." *Of Reformation in England*, *Complete Prose Works of John Milton* (New Haven: Yale University Press, 1953–1966)—hereafter referred to as *Complete Prose*—I, 528–529.

The Historical Genesis

[16] "On the New Forces of Conscience under the Long Parliament" (1647?) line 20.

[17] *A Second Defence of the English People*, Complete Prose, IV, 618–619.

[18] Ibid., 623–624.

[19] *The Reason of Church Government* II, Complete Prose, I, 822–823.

[20] *Of Education*, Complete Prose, II, 377–379.

[21] *Areopagitica*, Complete Prose, II, 558.

[22] St. Augustine, *The City of God*, II, 358: "Concerning man's first origin, our present life (if such a miserable estate can be called a life) does sufficiently prove that all his children were condemned in him."

[23] *The Christian Doctrine* I, xi, CE, XV, 181–183.

[24] Northrop Frye, *The Return of Eden: Five Essays on Milton's Epics* (Toronto, 1965) 109.

[25] *The Reason of Church Government* I, Complete Prose, I, 795.

[26] *A Defence of the People of England*, Complete Prose, IV, 317–318.

[27] Ibid., 457.

[28] Ibid., 317.

[29] *The Christian Doctrine* I, x, CE, XV, 115–117.

[30] *The Readie & Easie Way* (second ed., 1660) 9–10.

[31] *A Defence*, Complete Prose, IV, 466.

[32] *The Tenure of Kings and Magistrates*, Complete Prose, III, 202.

[33] Cf. Arthur Barker, *Milton and the Puritan Dilemma, 1641–1660*, (Toronto, 1942) 117 ff.

[34] *Tetrachordon*, Complete Prose, II, 661.

[35] Ibid.

[36] James Harrington, *The Commonwealth of Oceana*, intro. Henry Morley (London, 1887) 30.

II

The Humanistic Background

As A HUMANIST Milton is indebted in a major way to classical, medieval, and Renaissance traditions. But Milton's humanism is also marked by a staunch English Protestantism, which varies in its overt impact in his different works. Arnold Stein, in a sensitive and exhaustive study of the ideas underlying *Paradise Regained*, finds piety as the central theme. "Piety as the end of wisdom, and the relating of the end to the beginning, will be the subject of the whole dramatic process of the poem. . . . Piety is not only the cause, with other virtues, of real liberty, it is the one essential cause. . . ."[1] Stein contends that Milton is concerned with knowledge as wisdom in the service of piety—wisdom therefore relating to the individual's consciousness of God. Milton rejects as Stoic deception man's employment of natural virtues merely to project his image well before the community for its social approval. The Christian has to strike much deeper levels of reality. As Stein sees *Paradise Regained*, it constitutes a drama of the right kind of knowledge:

The Humanistic Background

The ultimate cause is knowledge and the ultimate knowledge is the knowledge of God. In this drama we have two competing theories of knowledge. Satan is the great empiric, the advocate of knowledge for power, knowledge derived externally from the impressions on sense, and worked up into patterns of practical reason reflecting human experience in the world, and among men. Christ's theory is the Platonic one of pure thought inaccessible to the senses, with judgment more important than perception.

Stein adds:

> The higher judgment, light from above reflected by the *Logos* in the soul, self-consciousness, unity of the self—these are the true bases for knowledge.[2]

Christ in *Paradise Regained* strongly supports the apparent simplicity of the Hebrew Scriptures, though there is a concealed irony in the fact that he often speaks in its support as a classical scholar. He discusses Roman history (Quintius, Fabricius, Curius, Regulus [II, 446]), the viciousness of the Emperor Tiberius (IV, 125 ff.), the Stoic philosophy (IV, 330 ff.). Roman and Athenian learning, all the oratory of Greece and Rome (IV, 360) cannot compare with the "majestic unaffected style" of the Hebrew prophets. He rejects, too, with an almost un-Miltonic ease, the impact of other cultures. Direct knowledge from on high is apparently all that matters:

> ... he who receives
> Light from above, from the fountain of light,
> No other doctrine needs. ...
> (IV, 288-290)

Milton's Christ, however, is sufficiently tolerant to make some allowance for the "light of Nature" as a source of goodness:

> Unless where moral virtue is express'd
> By light of Nature, not in all quite lost.
> (IV, 351–352)

Milton, in spite of the ambition of his greatest project (*Paradise Lost*), indicates an awareness of the possible limitations of human knowledge. "When we speak of knowing God," he says, "it must be understood with reference to the imperfect comprehension of man, for to know God as he really is far transcends the powers of man's thoughts, much more of perception. God therefore has made as full a revelation of himself as our minds can conceive or the weakness of our nature can bear."[3] The main preliminary for knowing something of the mind of God is a knowledge of the good of man and of the natural law. (This knowledge can be gained by the reading of Scripture, under the guidance of the Holy Spirit, written in the hearts of the believers.) "The Spirit which is given to us is a more certain guide than Scripture,"[4] he says, and nothing must prevail against the good of man. "Although indeed no ordinance human or from heaven can bind against the good of man; so that to keep them strictly against that end, is all one with to break them."[5] The good of man is defined by the written law (Scripture) and by the unwritten law of nature. "The unwritten law is no other than that law of nature given originally to Adam, and of which a certain remnant, or imperfect illumination, still dwells in the hearts of mankind; which, in the regenerate, under the influence of the Holy Spirit, is daily tending towards a renewal of the primitive brightness."[6]

The simplest guide to knowledge is Scripture, Milton argues when he follows the simpler levels of contemporary Puritanism, although he also often demonstrates greater subtleties. Almost inevitably, in this context, he rejects "the carnal supportment of tradition."[7] "We are expressly forbidden to pay any regard to

The Humanistic Background

human traditions, whether written or unwritten."[8] He believes that any Protestant will grant that the Scripture has more authority than the church.[9]

Though happily unfettered in his own time by later studies of the texts, by subsequent archaeological, historical, and linguistic discoveries, Milton is aware of scholarly standards in regard to Scripture. In *De Doctrina Christiana*, he explains the need for a knowledge of languages, inspection of the original texts, care in distinguishing between literal and figurative expressions and in recognizing anomalies of syntax. Thinking along these lines, he is careful to put the Spirit above the text and argues that the purpose of Providence in committing the writings of the New Testament to "such uncertain and variable guardianship" was to teach us by this very circumstance that the Spirit which is given to us is a more certain guide than Scripture.[10]

While Milton always emphasizes the individual interpretation of Scripture, he is very careful to insist that such interpretation must not be capricious individualism. Though "the liberty of investigating Scripture thoroughly is granted to all," Milton also adds, "neither therefore is it [the prophecy of Scripture] to be interpreted by the judgment of man, that is, by our own unassisted judgment, but by means of that Holy Spirit promised to all believers."[11] In *A Treatise of Civil Power*, Milton says that "to interpret convincingly to his own conscience none is able but himself guided by the Holy Spirit; and not so guided, none than he to himself can be a worse deceiver."[12]

But Milton can seem at times unguarded and theologically primitive in regard to Scripture. He enrolls himself among the number of those who acknowledge the word of God alone as the rule of faith.[13] "The Scriptures . . . partly by reason of their own simplicity, and partly through the divine illumination, are plain and perspicuous in all things necessary to salvation."[14] In

The Likeliest Means to Remove Hirelings, he observes, "Therefore are the Scriptures translated into every vulgar tongue, as being held in the main matters of belief and salvation, plain and easy to the poorest...."[15] The very essence of truth is plainness and brightness. Darkness and crookedness are our own. "The wisdom of God created understanding, fit and proportionate to truth the object, as the eye to the thing visible."[16]

Complete reliance on the Scripture, with complete freedom of interpretation, is for Milton the express essence of Protestantism. "First, it cannot be denied, being the main foundation of our protestant religion, that we of these ages, having no other divine rule or authority from without us warrantable . . . to ourselves and to such whose consciences we can so persuade, can have no other ground in matters of religion but only from the scriptures. And these being not possible to be understood without the divine illumination, which no man can know at all times to be in himself, much less to be at any time for certain in any other, it follows clearly, that no man or body of men in these times can be infallible judges or determiners in matters of religion to any other men's consciences but their own."[17]

The same man who exalts the power of reason, who is one of the greatest baroque artists and the last great Renaissance humanist, who is so greatly capable of shocking the orthodox, often hews to a simple, straight line on the scriptural level, forgetting the strict reservations he himself imposes. He does not merely dismiss "gay religions full of pomp and gold" (*Paradise Lost* I, 372). He goes further: "all corporeal resemblances of inward holiness and beauty are now past."[18] There is to be no clothing of the gospel: "he that will clothe the Gospel now, intimates plainly that the Gospel is naked, uncomely, that I may not say reproachful."[19]

The Humanistic Background

It is difficult to realize from a modern vantage point how literally the Scriptures were read in the seventeenth century, particularly those passages that were never intended to be factual narrative or history but poetry and allegory. Milton's apparently complete trust in the Scriptures is part of the cultural climate of his time. To support a position simply by scriptural quotation seems naive to us today, but not to Milton, nor to the men of his age. The Scriptures were supposed to contain infallible meaning, and sufficient understanding could be obtained from them by any person of good will cooperating with grace. However, he seems to hedge on the possibility that oneself or others may be wrong.

In the *Tetrachordon*, supporting divorce, Milton relies on four scriptural passages. The reader was supposed to accept Milton's interpretations of such passages as the right ones if his arguments proved sufficiently convincing. If the religious arguments met the standards of reason, the reader had no need to seek further. The possibility that one might be convinced by Milton's arguments but still remain skeptical about the merit or authenticity of the scriptural passages was never envisaged. Milton's use of Scripture as a means of knowledge has a curiously legal, even scientific air, especially in his prose, which is largely partisan. In poetry he attains a universality to which Scripture contributes a main metaphoric content, and the effect is quite different. Ironically and amusingly enough, he tried to prove a variety of unorthodox views about institutions and doctrines, all the way from marriage to the Trinity, by an *apparently* orthodox arrangement of a panoply of biblical quotations. As a result, his revolutionary ideas are presented in a very unrevolutionary way that failed to alarm many pious people.

The way in which Milton uses scriptural authority has received acerbic comment more than once. Thus one critic observes:

"When the Bible makes for his view, it speaks prescriptively; when it contradicts him, it is to be taken metaphorically."[20] If the Scriptures were read both literally and selectively, practically every Puritan position could find means of support. But Milton himself shows that many non-Puritan positions could find even more ingenious support through the same method.

Milton is suspicious in matters of religion of "the opinions of our forefathers or antiquity."[21] He often supports a predetermined position, sometimes an iconoclastic one, and is not looking for a synthesis of the potential wisdom that a variety of thinkers may have already contributed to a subject. While he is too well educated and scholarly not to reflect many of the traditions of the past, he obviously feels that it is the duty of a good Protestant to be antitraditional, even in the most traditional activity of all—the return to the Scriptures!

Milton's view of Scripture may throw light on the way in which we are intended to approach *Paradise Lost*. Traditionally, in dealing with Scripture, an artist was literal and exact. While he might extend the human situation, as in the medieval religious plays, he did not feel free to add to, or even interpret, what was literally set forth in the Bible. Probably Milton himself would not have felt free to extend interpretation in this sense if he had not sincerely believed that truth was available to the elect in the light of right reason and that, under the guidance of the Holy Spirit, one might get to know something of God's secret will and secret truth as well as God's will and truth clearly expressed to all. (It must be remembered, of course, that these are consistent, for Milton explicitly denies the possibility of God having two contradictory wills.)[22] The Spirit, instructing the "upright heart and pure," is the divine inspiration which Milton may have sincerely felt guided him to utter new truths, scriptural and *historical* truths, not merely imaginative and poetic truths. Milton may have felt that he was writing, in the Shakespearean sense, a "history" as distinct from a "tragedy." Milton might have taken a dim view of the now commonly held approach of contemporary critics that he is dealing with the "human condition," when he was really extending the meaning of Scripture. Basil Willey has reminded us of this possibility: "On the whole I think we must conclude that, whereas the pagan myths were to him but husks from which truth could be winnowed, the biblical events, if allegorical at all, were the deliberate allegories of God himself, and when God allegorizes he does not merely write or inspire parables. He also causes to happen the events which can be allegorically interpreted."[23]

THE MILLENNIAL IDEA

Milton's approach to scriptural interpretation contains elements of reserve and sophistication in spite of its fundamentalist and radical Protestant bent. On the one hand, he obviously thinks of a church, as traditionally accepted, as inhibiting and easily corruptible and never envisions it as a potentially dynamic organism capable of evolutionary growth. It might even be maintained that Milton thinks of God as writing—or at least inspiring—a book, rather than founding a church. Nevertheless, he is strongly against heresy-hunting, and he believes Scripture is subordinate to the good of man and to the guidance of the Holy Spirit.

Occasionally, however, Milton shares evangelical Christianity's involvement with certain obsessive ideas. One such idea was the widespread conviction that some sort of cosmic epiphany was at hand. He had shared the previous generation's conviction that a day of universal peace was at hand. It has been maintained that James I had thought of himself as a universal mediator destined to bring peace to Europe; he was to reestablish a Christian peace that would be reminiscent of the peace of Christ in the days of Caesar Augustus. Shakespeare's *Cymbeline* has been symbolically interpreted in the light of this idea. "When, towards the end of the play, Cymbeline emphatically announces, 'Well, my peace we will begin' (V, v, 458), the audience must have made a complex identification: the peace is to be the peace of the world at the time of Christ's birth, in which Britain participates, and also its attempted re-creation at the very time of the play's performance, with Jacobus Pacificus—who was a 'figure' of Augustus—on the throne."[24] Such an apocalyptic vision of universal Christian peace is also expressed in Shakespeare's Sonnet CVII, in which he speaks of "the prophetic soul / Of the wide world dreaming on things to come":

> Incertainties now proclaim themselves assured
> And peace proclaims olives of endless age.

A classical myth that served as a poetic image for this type of conviction, at the same time reinforcing it, was that of the goddess Astraea, associated with the return of the golden age. In his *Fourth Eclogue*, Virgil predicts the birth of a mysterious child who is to renew all things. At that time the stars in heaven return to the original position they had in the golden age. He refers in this connection to an original degeneration in the state of man. Man had been born to the golden age, but something went wrong, and we have successive stages of ensuing decay. In the golden age men and gods conversed freely together. (This is a rough parallel to the story in Genesis where God and Adam walked together enjoying the afternoon air.) The golden age slips into the silver age; then the gods converse only with particular men and only under the cover of darkness. Things go wrong in a still further degree, and ultimately we reach the age of iron, where envy, enmity, and war constitute man's major experience.

The Humanistic Background

Astraea, the virgin who represents truth and justice, once visited man and will be known to him again only with the return of the golden age. She is the key image in John Donne's first "Anniversary" poem, and furnishes a symbol easily associated with other ideas, particularly that of the Virgin Mary, and, consequently, with Christian holiness. Milton makes important use of this particular allegory in "On the Morning of Christ's Nativity":

> For if such holy Song
> Enwrap our fancy long,
>   Time will run back, and fetch the age of gold,
> And speckl'd vanity
> Will sicken soon and die,
>   And leprous sin will melt from earthly mold,
> And Hell itself will pass away,
> And leave her dolorous mansions to the peering day.
>
> Yea, Truth and Justice then
> Will down return to men,
>   Th' enamel'd Arras of the Rainbow wearing,
> And Mercy set between,
> Thron'd in Celestial sheen,
>   With radiant feet the tissued clouds down steering,
> And Heav'n as at some festival,
> Will open wide the Gates of her high Palace Hall.

In Book V of *The Faerie Queene* (i, st. iv–v), Sir Artegall, who symbolizes justice, has been reared by Astraea. His ultimate function is to restore the golden age, that of Gloriana herself, to bring back the symbolic Saturn who reigned in those halcyon days:

> For during Saturnes ancient raigne it's sayd
> That all the world with goodnesse did abound. . . .
>   (V, prologue, st. ix, 1–2)

The Elizabethan and Jacobean peace had never been established. The millennial idea—and some of its enthusiasts were prepared to accept slaughter and mayhem on route to its objective—had replaced it. While the idea was enthusiastically promoted by segments of radical Protestantism, it was by no means restricted to England. Europe, too, was absorbed with it. The millennium was assumed to be a period in which Christ would return to govern in person. Once the last terrible conflict with the enemies of God had been completed, Christ would judge all men and set up a kingdom of glory on earth with the saints at his side. The kingdom was to prevail, according to some interpretations, for a thousand years; then Satan was to be loosed for a short time. Other interpretations viewed the thousand years simply as a synecdoche for endless duration. A common version, as analyzed by William Haller, assumed that Daniel had seen the visions of the Four Monarchies: Babylon, Persia, Greece, and Rome. "The first three had been, and the fourth, in the person and power of the pope, was soon to be overthrown. There would be a time of great confusion—what more obvious than now or at any rate in the nearly approaching year of 1666 was the time meant?—and then the Fifth Monarchy, the kingdom of God on earth, would arise."[25] Revelation 21:1–3 was a basic text: "And I saw a new heaven and a new earth: for the first heaven and the first earth were passed away; and there was no more sea. And I, John, saw the holy city, new Jerusalem, coming down from God out of heaven, prepared as a bride adorned for her husband. And I heard a great voice out of heaven saying, Behold, the tabernacle of God is with men, and he will dwell with them, and they shall be his people, and God himself shall be with them, and be their God."

One aspect of the millennial idea was a concern to encourage the dispersion of the Jews. Some of the pertinent scriptural texts

The Humanistic Background

on this matter included Deuteronomy 28:64: "And the Lord shall scatter thee among all people, from the one end of the earth even to the other . . ."; Zechariah 8:22: "Yea, many people and strong nations shall come to seek the Lord of hosts in Jerusalem, and pray before the Lord"; Daniel 12:7: ". . . and when he shall have accomplished to scatter the power of the holy people, all these things shall be finished."

Both Jews and Christians were interested in seeing that this dispersion be historically accomplished as a prelude to the return of the chosen people to the New Jerusalem—in a literal and not merely a metaphorical sense. Rabbi Menasseh Ben Israel (1604–1657) was invited by Oliver Cromwell to come from Amsterdam and found a Jewish community in London. Menasseh was the head of a congregation in Holland whose members were skilled in the shipbuilding trade. Cromwell valued Jewish immigrations in these terms alone, for England was to become increasingly competitive with Holland in this field. But it is probably that the main ground for the invitation was religious. Menasseh himself was convinced of the imminent return of the Jews to the Holy Land according to Messianic promise, but the fulfillment of this first depended on recalling the Jews from *all* lands. First of all, of course, they had to be in all lands. It was assumed that even among the Indians of America, remnants of the Lost Tribes could be found, but England, located in the northernmost part of the settled world, had had no Jews living in it for three hundred and fifty years. This argument Menasseh had developed in the *Esperanza de Israel*, translated into *The Hope of Israel* (1650). The work came to the attention of Cromwell and deeply impressed English Puritans.

This determination to bring about a literal fulfillment of a biblical prophecy was part of a widespread European movement. As early as 1643, for example, Isaac de la Peyrère in his *Du*

Rappel des Juifs had suggested that Louis XIV of France take a hand in conquering Palestine from the Turks and Arabs in order to settle the Jews in their promised land, because the recall of the Jews by God was impending. Certain dates were considered pivotal in the fulfillment of such prophecies. The Christian dates, based on the year of our Lord, were considered successively as 1618, 1623, 1654, 1666. The Jewish dates, based on the chronology of "since the creation of the world," were 1648, 1666, 1695, 1706.

The extent to which Milton committed himself to the millennial idea can be gauged by one of his most eloquent passages in *Of Reformation in England* (1641), a passage echoing the theme of Revelation 22:5: "And there shall be no night there; and they need no candle, neither light of the sun; for the Lord God giveth them light: and they shall reign forever and ever." Milton thinks of England as a great and warlike nation pressing on hard to that "high and happy emulation to be found in the soberest, wisest, and most Christian people at that day, when thou, the eternal and shortly expected King, shall open the clouds to judge the several Kingdoms of the world, and distributing national honors and rewards to religious and just commonwealths, shall put an end to all earthly tyrannies, proclaiming thy universal and mild monarchy through heaven and earth. . . ."[26]

Some interpreters of Milton find his later work tinged with melancholy because the millennial dream was not fulfilled. They believe that even *Paradise Lost* is concerned not with the Second Coming but with things as they are, the human condition as the reader must know it. "Relegated to that recital which for Adam concerns only a distant future and for the reader an equally remote past, the Second Coming is cramped into the farthest perspective of a vast and tangled panorama."[27]

The Humanistic Background

MILTON'S CONCEPT OF RIGHT REASON

Milton makes certain broad identifications in theory, whatever tensions or dilemmas they may create in practice, between the law of God, the law of nature,[28] and *right reason*. He tells Salmasius, "I now believe, as I have always done, Salmasius, that the law of God does most closely agree with the law of nature."[29] In *De Doctrina Christiana* he observes: "Seeing, however, that man was made in the image of God, and had the whole law of nature so implanted and innate in him, that he needed no precept to enforce its observance, it follows, that if he received any additional commands, whether respecting the tree of knowledge, or the institution of marriage, these commands formed no part of the law of nature, which is sufficient of itself to teach whatever is agreeable to right reason, that is to say, whatever is intrinsically good."[30] Milton is a Socratic optimist about the function of right reason, and one critic has said, "Milton thinks so highly of his reason, has such a trust in his intellect, that he wants reason to be a mistress absolute in herself."[31]

In Book V of *Paradise Lost*, Milton makes a succinct analysis of his doctrine of reason. The lesser faculties of the soul serve reason as chief. The concept of reason as commanding the balanced relationship of the various faculties of man's soul derives from Plato, who stated that "the forbidding principle is derived from reason, and that which bids and attracts from passion and disease."[32] Plato contrasts the rational principle of the soul with the irrational or appetitive. He further divides the irrational principle into the concupiscent and irascible. The irascible faculty, when not corrupted by faulty education, aids reason. The temperate man is one in whom these elements are in harmony:

> For the just man does not permit the several elements within him to interfere with one another, or any of them to do the

work of others—he sets in order his own inner life, and is his own master and his own law, and at peace with himself; and when he has bound together the three principles within him, which may be compared to the higher, lower, and middle notes of the scale, and the intermediate intervals—when he has bound all these together, and is no longer many, but has become one entirely temperate and perfectly adjusted nature, then he proceeds to act, if he has to act, whether in a matter of property, or in the treatment of the body, or in some affair of politics or private business; always thinking and calling that which preserves and cooperates with this harmonious condition, just and good action, and the knowledge which presides over it, wisdom, and that which at any time impairs the condition, he will call unjust action, and the opinion which presides over it ignorance.[33]

The rational faculty, the function of which is to direct the will in terms of the harmonious relationship thus described by Plato, is not, however, exactly coterminous with *right* reason. Professor Douglas Bush speaks of the principle of right reason as a Stoic concept so long a part of Christian thought that its origin was half forgotten. With varying Platonic, Aristotelian, or Stoic emphasis, it is a concept basic to Christian humanism at all times. In seventeenth-century England, Milton and the Cambridge Platonists particularly stressed this idea. Right reason does not mean reason in the modern sense, nor does it mean simply religious conscience:

> It is a kind of rational and philosophic conscience which distinguishes man from the beasts and which links man with man and with God. This faculty was implanted by God in all men, Christian and heathen alike, as a guide to truth and conduct. Though its effectual workings may be obsured by sin, it makes man, in his degree, like God; it enables him, within limits, to understand the purpose of a God who is perfect reason as well as perfect justice, goodness, and love.[34]

The Humanistic Background

Bush lists some of the elements in the thought of the Cambridge Platonists in regard to right reason. First, there is a recognition of a divine unity of the world and a divine unity of truth, natural and supernatural. Another element is an optimism in regard to the nature of man, in contrast to Augustinian, Lutheran, Calvinistic, and Hobbesian views. Balancing this optimism, however, is a chastening recognition of man's vulnerability. Generally, the Cambridge Platonists opposed religious "enthusiasm" and stressed the active Christian life:

> Right reason does not turn away from nature as evil, still less does it set up nature against "artificial" restraints of religion and morality. Both attitudes would be impossible because God and nature are one—which does not mean a pantheistic confusion of creation with the Creator and an irreligious worship of life and flux. What we do have is a fundamental opposition to Calvinism on the one hand and naturalism on the other.[35]

God himself supremely manifests right reason. What God is to the world, reason is to the soul. One of the ways in which Milton justifies the ways of God to man is by insistence on man's rational freedom of moral choice.

> But God left free the Will, for what obeys
> Reason, is free, and Reason he made right,
> But bid her well beware, and still erect,
> Lest by some fair appearing good surpris'd
> She dictate false, and misinform the Will
> To do what God expressly hath forbid.
> *(Paradise Lost* IX, 351–356)

In the quotation above we have an unresolved ambiguity that would bear on any interpretation of *Paradise Lost*. If, in the line "and Reason he made right," no emphasis is placed on the word *made*, reason has the connotation of the moral law of the universe that was made right for all time. If emphasis is placed on *made*, the implication would be that reason was made right but did not continue to stay right. Any given rational faculty in a particular instance "participates" to a greater or lesser degree in the universal, though Milton suggests in his phrasing that originally the participation amounted to absolute identity.

In his adaptation of the classical principle of the rational soul, Milton inherits the traditional dilemma in the relationship of classical reason to Christian grace. Any anthology of quotations from Milton on this subject would show a mixed pattern. In his exaltation of reason, he is much more of a medieval Thomist than he would have suspected; in other passages, particularly in references to the Holy Spirit guiding the true believer, he is an Augustinian illuminist.[36] He is poles apart from Roger Ascham, who, in *The Schoolmaster* (1570), clearly puts the will above the mind: "There be in man two special things: man's will, man's mind. Where will inclineth to goodness, the mind is bent to truth. Where will is carried from goodness to vanity, the mind is soon drawn from truth to false opinion. And so the readiest way to entangle the mind with false doctrine is first to entangle the will to wanton living." Milton trusts the human intelligence, with few reservations: "But all agree that while the human Intellect shines forth as the lord and governor of all other faculties, it guides and illuminates with its radiance the Will also, which would else be blind, and the Will shines with a borrowed light, even as the moon doth."[37]

But is grace a principle of intelligence which illuminates the mind from the outside? Is it the power of universal intelligence actuating the successive, transitory minds of men? Or is the active intelligence, as Aquinas indicated, the very essence of the soul and the root of human responsibility and liberty?[38] Is the study of Scripture to rely on divine illumination or on the

The Humanistic Background

exercise of the trained human intelligence? Is there an additional supernatural machinery enabling man to know in addition to the machinery innate in him?

It would be difficult to state exactly what Milton's thought would be relative to such questions. When he responds to the self-sufficiency of Hellenic tradition in regard to reason, Milton does look upon reason as a mistress absolute in herself. But when it comes to the things of God, the mysteries of revealed truth, then reason has to yield to something higher:

> . . . Heav'n is for thee too high
> To know what passes there; be lowly wise:
> Think only what concerns thee and thy being. . . .
> (Paradise Lost VIII, 172–174)

Then what Arnold Stein terms piety—the relationship of a reverent son toward an instructing father—becomes the characteristic role of right reason, its proper role in relationship to the true nature of things.[39] Knowledge, like food, has to be governed by the laws of temperance (Paradise Lost VII, 126–130); God's secrets should be admired rather than scanned (Paradise Lost VII, 71–75); we should not be concerned with matters hid (Paradise Lost VIII, 167). For Milton an obvious characteristic of right reason is the acceptance of limitation, even in regard to knowledge. At this point some readers may feel that, in contrast to many of his expressed enthusiasms about the role of reason and knowledge, he veers too much in the direction of simple piety:

> . . . but to know
> That which before us lies in daily life,
> Is the prime Wisdom. . . .
> (Paradise Lost VIII, 192–194)

Anything more "is fume / Or emptiness." It might facetiously be asked to what extent the speculations in *Paradise Lost* itself constitute what lies before us in our daily life, and whether these speculations constitute fume and emptiness. Although he is writing in a special context (Adam's response to the instructing Raphael), Milton's doctrine here is somewhat inconsistent with positions stated elsewhere, and, whether he likes it or not, Milton in presenting the Fall of man comes up squarely against the problem of knowledge again, implicit in the concept of right reason, revelation, and temptation.

THE DEGREE OF PURITAN INFLUENCE

For many years the tendency in Miltonic criticism has been to stress Milton as a humanist rather than as a Puritan. Most readers are certainly more impressed by his humanistic role, but the Puritan influence cannot realistically be altogether disregarded. As it has already been mentioned, this influence is shown, for example, in Milton's frequently unreserved support of the Scriptures; his fleeting enthusiasm about the millenial idea; the concept of the elect as possessing rather than earning virtue and the view of temptation as a confirmation of—rather than a threat to—virtue (though these two approaches are only characteristic of *Comus* and *Paradise Regained*); the idea of life as tension, hard work, thrift, under the direction of an admired taskmaster.

However, Milton often veers away from Puritan positions, particularly theological ones, while still maintaining the basic overtones of evangelical Christianity. On the whole, he rejects the doctrine of essential depravity through original sin, though occasional passages, including a key one in *Paradise Lost* (X, 823–827) may point in an opposite direction. He rejects predestination with its implication that grace is arbitrarily and capriciously bestowed. He insists on free will as characteristic of human

The Humanistic Background

dignity. Not only does Milton take a more optimistic view of the nature of man than is customary in Calvinistic theology, he thinks of salvation as potential for all, without exception: Christ died for men in general, for the Scripture offers salvation and eternal life equally for all.[40]

Late Augustinian (Calvinist, Lutheran) thought emphasized the primacy of the will over the intellect. While its theology was emphatically spiritual in its emphasis on grace and in the Platonic sense, it was not normally Socratic in its approach to knowledge (though Milton normally is). On the question of the primacy of the will, too, Milton is far from adhering strictly to the Puritan line.

The Puritan stress on the power of the will, in the process of election, justification, sanctification, glorification, is rather paradoxical. One might logically expect that a determinist, certain of the ultimate outcome of events, could afford to relax. But it is in his conduct and in the fruits of activity that the Puritan finds assurance of his election. Any serious deviation from his ethical uprightness would indicate to him that he had never been written in the Book of Life. One critic observes, "Puritanism is a religion of the will, of the individual conscience, almost (one might say) of self-reliance. If the Puritan cannot make his peace with God out of the scrupulousness of his own soul, there is no one who can do it for him."[41] Though Puritans wrote numbers of introspective spiritual diaries, they did not emphasize contemplation (though this is certainly not true of Milton). Contemplation tended to be associated with the survival of a haughty pagan classicism or with plain idleness; the course of salvation is marked by work and industry. Hilaire Belloc once observed that "since conduct and action, though availing nothing to attain the free gift of salvation, are a proof that the gift has been accorded, what is rejected as a means is resumed as a consequence, and the Puritan flings himself into practical activities with the demonic energy of one who, all doubts allayed, is conscious that he is a sealed and chosen vessel."[42]

In emphasizing the will, the Puritan tends to place a much higher value on what results from personal achievement than on what might be regarded as a free gift of God. Many Christian theologies agree that man is freely given immortality of soul, that he possesses a potential intelligence in the natural order which can reach the threshold of the highest truth, that through the redemption he has been adopted as a brother of Jesus Christ, as a son of the Father. Above all he experiences the ultimately wonderful truth, that of his being, that he *is*, and that he *is* without centuries of planning and premeditation on his part. Adam, in Book VIII of *Paradise Lost*, in describing his creation expresses a good deal of this sense of wonder. Theologians traditionally thought of these matters as free gifts. They would seem to be of primary importance, especially the free gift of being; what a man achieves through his own energy and industry, while important, is derivative from what he did not earn but was freely given. Puritan theology tended to minimize man in terms of his ontology—what he intrinsically is; he is exalted in terms of what he makes himself. Milton gives the impression that he shared at times this psychological emphasis of Puritanism, even though he did not adhere strictly to the thought behind it. He could respond more easily to the rigorous eye of the great taskmaster than to the relaxed babe at Bethlehem.

The passionately personal, intimate religious note is fairly rare in Milton (though "Lycidas" might be cited as an exception), and this lack may be due more to the Puritan environment than to anything in Milton's own temperament. Milton is primarily interested in principle—private and, more particularly, public ethic. Milton's God is a public figure but not a devotional one;

The Humanistic Background

he is administrator, philosopher, magistrate. Louis Martz has noted, "Students of English Puritanism have often remarked upon the small part which the person and humanity of Christ played in Puritan writings of the sixteenth and seventeenth centuries."[43] The medieval mystical tradition that the spiritual life is primarily the preparation of one's self for relationship to a *person*, that sin is a rejection of a person rather than a failure in attaining an image of perfection, yields to the Puritan concept of a righteous and just man who has an elect status. The concept of such a just man permits a spiritual happiness—the possession of a good conscience—without the need for great emotional warmth. The medieval person-to-person note was not simply a matter of primitive religious art. It was also a cast of mind, marked by such a sacrament as confession and penance, by such a doctrine as purgatory—both of which were rejected by Protestant tradition. It is true that the sense of real temptation and real remorse is convincingly communicated in *Paradise Lost*, but even there the tragic impact is largely restricted to the awareness of the enormity of the moral consequences contingent on the Fall rather than revealing lyrically any despair over loss of the personal relationship between the soul and God. The third person of the *ménage à trois* is temporarily removed and is replaced by the more abstract image of Providence, and "the world was all before them."

Obviously there were aspects of Christianity to which Puritanism was not psychologically attuned. The shepherd rejoicing at finding the lost sheep, personal devotionalism, Christmas, and the return of the prodigal son are among the subjects not emphasized. Puritans tended to view the Incarnation as simply an incident in the Redemption (even Milton's "On the Morning of Christ's Nativity" is primarily about the Redemption and its effects upon human history). What the Puritans overlooked is that the Incarnation makes possible knowledge of a person in contrast to knowledge about a person gained through intellectual processes. St. Bernard of Clairvaux had argued in the *De diligendo Deo* (1127/35) that God became incarnate precisely in order to open a way of access to the unsearchable ways of God, who otherwise would have remained entirely hidden from us. The idea of a Great Chain of Being which Milton accepts (*Paradise Lost* V, 469 ff.) has, in one sense, the effect of only apparently foreshortening the distance between God and man, for the difference between the finite and the infinite is one not simply of degree but also of kind. To unite finite being with infinite being demands more than Milton's "gradual scale sublim'd"; such an epiphany demands a mystical leap, and actually only the Incarnation could justify this foreshortening.

Milton thinks of men as ascending through spiritual stages to the angelic level ("Till body up to spirit work," *Paradise Lost* V, 476). Rather than an angelic destiny for man, St. Bernard envisages a union of the divine and human, in which the human remains true to its own nature and does not become angelic. The effect of *excessus* (cf. the seventeenth-century "ecstasy") is to cause him who loves to have nothing of his own to will of *his own* will. Circumscribed on all sides by God he is as air flooded with light or as iron liquified with fire. But this passion through ecstasy does not involve the soul's destruction. For the substance of the soul remains intact and the *excessus* confirms it in its own true nature.

It is instructive to contrast the views of a Platonic Christian like Milton with those of an incarnational Christian like St. Bernard. St. Bernard's ladder of ascent in *De diligendo Deo* avoids a certain nonhuman, rather frigid aspect of Platonic Christianity. Where the Greek ladder of perfection is accepted, as suggested in Plato's *Symposium*, the soul ultimately moves from the material world to the contemplation of the divine archetypes; the rungs of the ladder beneath the perfection-seeking soul are kicked away. St. Bernard's objective lies not so much in seeking an abstract relationship of perfection but, rather, in perfecting and increasing in depth a relation that already exists. The monk, having reached a mystical relationship with God, does not forget or forsake humanity. His *two-way* ladder also returns to earth, but he no longer sees man with an egoistic love. He now sees men from God's point of view, as it were, through God's eyes—in other words, with much more compassion than before undergoing this spiritual discipline. Monks were not to become angels. Rather, Christ became man, accepting human limitations, and to be truly human in the Christlike sense was man's highest honor. Man in beatitude still remains essentially human.

Milton himself observes that at times nothing serves better than self-esteem based on the just and right (*Paradise Lost* IX, 335). This self-esteem St. Bernard would see as the result of natural necessity. Man's self-love in this sense does not mean that he prefers himself to God. There can be precedence without preference; such love is first in the order of experience but not first in the order of values. This love has to be transformed. For St. Bernard the image of God in the soul is the *freedom* of human nature itself. (Milton would have relished this idea.) But the image is not the same thing as the similitude or likeness to God. The image is constant, but the *likeness* has to be achieved. Love of self can become the great enemy to God in the sense that God is left out of the picture, but the ultimate achievement of charity is the highest kind of self-love—to love oneself as God loves one.

Milton might have been even richer than he is, if he had been better acquainted with the refinements of medieval thought rather than its "scholastic trash."[44] But Milton—even if one might feel that there are some blank areas in him because of his Puritan environment—is much larger than the culture amid which he moved. A certain kind of medieval tradition, in contrast to Puritanism and Platonic classicism, would have provided the insight that sin is a transgression against a loved *person* even more than it is a transgression against justice, against an ordered universe, against salvation itself.[45]

MILTON AS A CHRISTIAN HUMANIST

But the fact remains that, in so far as a humanist is primarily interested in the knowledge of what is human, Milton is in the forefront of humanist tradition. He emphasizes the divine because the divine guarantees what is human. He is not a mystic inflamed with the rapture of God; nor does he, psychologically or otherwise, make the divine serve purely human purposes. It is simply that his focus of interest lies in the human situation, even if he may have the role of inspired prophet. But the integrity of what is human depends upon the support and nourishment derived from something still higher—in fact, upon what is highest. If the seventeenth-century poet could not love so much, loved he not honor more, neither could the humanist love man so much, loved he not justice more—for the religious poet, justice embodied in the person of God.

Milton's humanist position accords with the medieval concept that man, even if fallen, is the center of the interests of the created universe. Even Satan himself expresses this concept, in thinking of the stars of heaven shining *for* man:

> Light above Light, for thee alone, as seems
> In thee concentring all thir precious beams
> Of sacred influence: As God in Heav'n
> Is Centre, yet extends to all, so thou

The Humanistic Background

> Centring receiv'st from all those Orbs; in thee,
> Not in themselves, all thir known virtue appears
> Productive in Herb, Plant, and nobler birth
> Of Creatures animate with gradual life
> Of Growth, Sense, Reason, all summ'd up in Man.
> (*Paradise Lost* IX, 105–113)

Like Sir Thomas More's Utopians, Milton believed in a happiness that combined rationalistic knowledge with religious principles. In *Prolusions VII* Milton argues: "If then learning is our guide and leader in the search after happiness, if it is ordained and approved by almighty God, and most conformable to His glory, surely it cannot but bring the greatest blessings upon those who follow after it."[46] Statements in the *Utopia* are practically interchangeable with this. The Utopians defined virtue as living according to nature. "We have been ordained, they say, by God to this end. To follow nature is to follow the dictate of reason in what we seek and avoid. The first dictate of reason is to love and revere the Divine majesty, to whom we owe what we are and whatever happiness we can reach."[47] The Utopians count among the highest pleasures knowledge and the delight which comes from the contemplation of truth. In admiring nature, man admires the architect of nature. "He has exposed this machine of the universe to man's view because man alone is able to contemplate it, and therefore a casual observer and eager admirer of His workmanship is dearer to Him than a dull and unmoved being who looks upon this great spectacle like an animal incapable of thought."[48] Milton could have said all these things—and did, in slightly different language.

On basic universals, Milton is in direct line with the earlier Christian humanists of the Renaissance. Even under the surface of bitter political and sectarian controversy, his basic humanistic concerns burn steadily, only their excess of glory obscured. Those concerns relate to universal ideas and values, for it is typical of the humanistic mind to be unsatisfied with contingents and particulars. It seeks a universality of truth which can synthesize and unite all particular truths, a truth which can attract all men by the light of reason and, ultimately, by the light of grace.

The Renaissance humanist was also a classical scholar. The term *humanist* originally applied to a teacher of Greek and Latin. Since the teacher was also a commentator on texts, especially those of Plato, he inevitably gravitated to the field of moral philosophy. At first, a casual reader might be amazed by Milton's statement placing Edmund Spenser in a higher category as a moral teacher (that is, a philosopher) than St. Thomas Aquinas or Duns Scotus.[49] But such an evaluation is easily explicable in terms of the Renaissance context, where philosophy is viewed less as a precise intellectual system than as a means of inspiration to meet the contingencies of life (we may recall Shakespeare's Friar Laurence's "adversity's sweet milk, philosophy").[50] Edmund Spenser had declined to address a coterie of scholarly friends in Dublin on the benefits to be derived from a study of moral philosophy because a projected work entitled *The Faerie Queene* was to fulfill the purpose. It was taken for granted that a sage and serious poet was an expert in the field of moral philosophy.

The emphasis on philosophy as a source of morality and inspiration made an alliance with poetry easy and natural. Spenser's concept of the poetic vocation, as uttered by his spokesman E. K. in *The Shepheardes Calender*, was "no art, but a divine gift and heavenly instinct, not to be gotten by labor and learning, but adorned with both and poured into the wit by a certain enthusiasm and celestial inspiration."[51] These could have been Milton's own words.

The Humanistic Background

Sir Philip Sidney thinks of Scholastic philosophers as casting largesse as they go of "definitions, divisions, distinctions." But it is never quite clear what specific elements of Scholasticism are being rejected. The Renaissance demanded a new idiom, a philosophical language with more imaginative and emotional appeal, and the dry, categorical discourse of the medievalists did not suit its temperament. In Thomas More and Francis Bacon, who anticipate the practical advantages of scientific research, many of philosophy's subtle ramifications seem frivolous and irrelevant. More's Utopians had not "yet invented the subtle distinctions and hypotheses which have been so cleverly worked out in our trifling schools of logic."[52] The Utopians, albeit unversed in Scholastic logic, "thoroughly understood the course of the stars and the motions of the heavenly spheres. They have contrived various instruments for computing exactly the course and position of the sun, moon, and the other heavenly bodies visible in their part of the sky."[53] Milton, like More, is deeply suspicious of Scholasticism, particularly as it pertains to religion. He objects to "scholastical trash" and "scholastic sophistry,"[54] in his fundamentalist Protestant fear of "vague cogitations and subtleties."[55]

But the main objection to Scholasticism had been aesthetic, rather than intellectual. Even when the humanist found Plato and Neoplatonism inspiring, and Scholasticism revolting, he had absorbed and maintained from his own educational background a great deal of the Scholastic tradition. The medieval tradition of the debate, for example, served Milton well. In spite of his own extremely strong convictions, more than once bordering on eccentricity, he is always cognizant of the need to dramatize the opposition as fairly as possible. Even if he loads the debate, the poet is always aware of the main points that can be made against him. This medieval instrument of education is evident throughout Milton—from the academic exercises to the dramatizations of Satan, Comus, Dalila. Critics have not been wanting who maintain that Milton is basically sympathetic to Satan, that Comus has strong points to make, and that Dalila has some justification. Though he found Spenser the most inspiring philosopher, Milton indirectly owes something to the Aquinas tradition of marshalling all the arguments for a proposition, all the arguments against, followed by a summary and a decision.[56]

Though it might be argued that Scholasticism had been poetically uninspiring (we must remember, however, that it served Dante well), though it might be alleged that it was overrationalistic, it believed in definition, debate, and disciplined verbal formulation. The latter are also characteristic of Milton's work and are at times distasteful to critics, as in the allegation, for example, that Milton's God talks like a school divine.[57] Milton, despite his overt rejection of Scholasticism, certainly retains a major share of its semantics. Moreover, he often goes back to classical sources that are also a force in Scholasticism itself. Cicero affords a good example. "Cicero, as a lawyer and statesman, was especially interested in the Stoic equation of God, Nature, Reason, and Law. In the first book of *De Legibus* he lays a solid foundation for the philosophy of law that was later to be articulated by St. Thomas Aquinas and Richard Hooker."[58] Many of the major postulates of Scholasticism are native to Milton. Basil Willey's description of the broad outlines of the thinking of Aquinas would be interchangeable with that of Milton:

> St. Thomas sees the universe as a hierarchy of creatures ordered to the attainment of perfection in their several kinds. All things proceed from God; and God is not only the ground of their being but also the Supreme Good with which all seek to be reunited. God created the world so that he might communicate himself more fully; as First Mover (the "unmoved mover" of Aristotle) he impels all creatures

to desire him. Love is thus "the deepest spring of all causality".... God not only created but continually sustains the world, and governs it directly by the eternal laws and indirectly through (for instance) the angels, and through the celestial bodies upon whose motions all terrestrial motion depends.[59]

Certain basic humanistic assumptions in Milton's philosophy underlie most Renaissance views: man's possession of right reason, originally perfect and even now participating in varying degrees with the moral law of the universe; the consonance of right reason with the law of nature, the law of nations, and with the true meaning of the Scriptures.

THE HELLENIC INFLUENCE

Nearly all commentators on the high Hellenic art, whether in literature, sculpture, or architecture, have stressed the effect of nobility that the Greeks obtained by a sense of form that suggests repose, the eternal element amid the transient—an essence of beauty that is realistic and recognizable by all, yet skillfully avoiding the one detail too many that would compromise the work and bring it into too close a contact with the purely vulgar and representational. The Greek artistic skill consists in being close to experience and still achieving the finesse which has been the constant aim of abstract art. Greek sculpture of a woman looks like a woman, even like a particular woman, and yet the deepest impression that the sculptor leaves with us is the living and breathing essence of woman as a universal image. Walter Pater thought of Greek sculpture in terms of "pure form"—"a little of suggested motion, and much of pure light on its gleaming surfaces, with pure form—only these. And it gains much more than it loses by this limitation to its own distinguishing motives; it unveils man in the repose of its unchanging characteristics."[60] Milton writes about one Edward King in "Lycidas," but he tells us mainly about universal man. At the same time the individual Edward King is not lost in, or sacrificed to, the more universal theme. Greek art is realistic but magnificently avoids the limitations of realism. It is idealistic without ceasing to be human, and this is true of Milton at his best.

This special sense of form is related to the Greek emphasis on measurement, on the right proportion of things. Greek thinking is preoccupied with ratio, with numbers, and with the relationships of music. Everything has to be rightly proportioned, properly balanced. It is the function of reason and temperance to observe these proper boundaries and relationships. A key idea in all of Plato's thinking is that of harmony. The Greeks think of the great universe, the macrocosm, as comprising a cosmic harmony in which all the parts join in the one harmonious music of the spheres. Man, the microcosm or the lesser world, reflects in his own being the harmony of the universe as a whole. The secret of virtue is proper knowledge—that is a knowledge of relationships, of proper proportions. Greek tragedy tells of what happens when harmony is attacked, when disproportion is created, and of how overweening self-confidence (a violation of "know thyself" and a denial of "nothing in excess") leads to insanity and self-destruction.

Milton could not have been so enthusiastic about Edmund Spenser without being enthusiastic about the central philosophical point in *The Faerie Queene*, the classical theory of moderation. The Aristotelian concept of virtue was that of a mean between extremes—between excesses, on the one hand, and deficiencies, on the other. Constantly Spenser allegorizes the virtues by depicting the excesses and deficiencies that are opposed to them. Aristotle, in the *Nicomachean Ethics*, illustrates the point of view central to Spenser and Hellenic humanism:

The Humanistic Background

That moral virtue is a mean, then, and in what sense it is so, and that it is a mean between two vices, the one involving excess, the other deficiency, and that it is such because its character is to aim at what is intermediate in passion and action, has been sufficiently stated. Hence it is no easy task to be good. For in everything it is no easy task to find the middle, e.g., to find the middle of the circle is not for every one but for him who knows; so, too, anyone can get angry —that is easy—or give or spend money; but to do this to the right person, to the right extent, at the right time, with the right motive, and in the right way, *that* is not for everyone, nor is it easy; wherefore goodness is both rare and laudable and noble.[61]

Adam in *Paradise Lost* goes through a process of Aristotelian instruction at the hands of the Archangel Raphael, who informs him:

> But Knowledge is as food, and needs no less
> Her Temperance over Appetite. . . .
> (*Paradise Lost* VII, 126–127)

The emphasis on moderation is most characteristically classical. Moderation in regard to the appetite for knowledge is a logical development of this doctrine but is distinctly Miltonic. That Milton is classical in style can be endlessly demonstrated, but there have been writers who were classical in style without being classical in temperament. Milton has a genuinely classical cast of mind, and this is superbly illustrated by his enchantment with the idea of harmony based upon the principle of moderation.

In various sections of his works Milton alludes to the music of the spheres.[62] In his early *Prolusions II* he speaks of the lark soaring up into the clouds at dawn and of the nightingale passing lonely hours of the night in song, in order that they might harmonize their songs to the heavenly music.[63] He believes that there is a symphony of celestial bodies giving forth a perpetual concert, a harmonious praise to God. In "On the Morning of Christ's Nativity," we are told of the angelic choruses that sounded on earth at the creation but were never heard again, after the sin of Adam, until the morning of the Nativity.

The *musica mundana* (primarily "sphere" music) holds the universe together but is itself an imperfect copy of the music of the angels, of the heavenly muses. At the moment of Christ's birth the original music replaces the copy, and the physical sphere music is summoned to be heard and to be in perfect accord with the *prima musica*—"Ring out ye Crystal spheres . . . Make up full consort to th'Angelic symphony."[64]

The idea of the music of the spheres is a very ancient one, going back to Plato and Pythagoras. Music, as conceived by the Greeks, was an important ingredient in all of man's relationships to the external world. The earth itself is full of "natural" music, and man, the microcosm, should respond to music since even insensible things do. Through music Linus and Orpheus tamed beasts and birds, moved rocks, and checked streams. All things are governed by harmony, and it is here that audible music becomes significant to man, since it can, in a sense, lead him to the divine. The soul of man is naturally sympathetic to music, and music, by regularizing the motion of the body, can even give physical health. Robert Burton says of music in the *Anatomy of Melancholy* that it "is so powerful a thing that it ravisheth the soul . . . corporal tunes pacify our incorporeal soul . . . [music] carries it beyond itself, helps elevate, extend it."[65]

We may go so far as to say that the succession of allusions to the music of the spheres reaches a high point in Milton's poetry. In *Prolusions II* he combines two classical traditions, that of the return of the golden age and that of the music of the spheres. Milton says that it seems to be the consequence of the insolence

The Humanistic Background

of the robber Prometheus that so many evils were brought upon man, and at that time we were deprived of that facility which we shall never be permitted to enjoy again as long as we wallow in sin and are brutalized by our animal desires. How can we, whose spirits are warped earthward and are defective in every heavenly element, be sensitive to that celestial sound? If our hearts were as pure, as chaste, as snowy as that of Pythagoras was, our ears would be filled with that supremely lovely music of the wheeling stars. Then indeed all things would return to the age of gold, where we should be immune to pain and should enjoy the blessings of a peace that the gods themselves might envy. Milton states this doctrine most explicitly in the *Arcades*:

> ... then listen I
> To the celestial Sirens' harmony,
> That sit upon the nine infolded Spheres
> And sing to those that hold the vital shears
> And turn the Adamantine spindle round,
> On which the fate of gods and men is wound.
> Such sweet compulsion doth in music lie,
> To lull the daughters of Necessity,
> And keep unsteady Nature to her law,
> And the low world in measur'd motion draw
> After the heavenly tune, which none can hear
> Of human mold with gross unpurged ear. ...
> (62–73)

The idea of harmony is one of future vision rather than of present reality. It belongs to the ideal world. The highest Greek art touched this vision. It memorialized, under the aspect of eternity, a high moment of human beauty, of human grace. It reminds us of a human possibility as well as of the human situation. Man is habituated to flux and change, but he has a dream of permanence, of stability, of the "heavenly tune."

THE THEME OF GLORY

One word that belongs especially to the Renaissance in the sense that it became particularly emotive at that period is the word *glory*. Edmund Spenser did not find any explanation necessary in making glory the governing virtue of *The Faerie Queene*. Glory is also among the leading themes of *Paradise Lost*. Today the word has no obvious connotation for us. Theologically many of us have been instructed in the concept of the glory of God; we have been taught that somehow we should participate in this and be grateful for it. But modern life has so emphasized the contingent and the particular that the phrase now lacks emotive force. Glory is a key word, nevertheless, in Milton. Rationalistic as he may appear at times, Milton recognizes wonder, mystery, incomprehensibility. "God must be styled by us wonderful and incomprehensible,"[66] he states. It is for this very reason that "God has condescended to accomodate himself to our capacities and has lowered himself to our level."[67] Apparently the effulgence, the epiphany of the divine harmony of the universe, is symbolized by *glory*. Glory points to the blaze of being dependent on unity—glory in the sense of a vibrant beauty emanating through all things.

The word had had a long heritage running from classical through medieval times, often with the connotation of reputation and honor as well as that of the splendor of being. Glory for the Greeks was a kind of immortality—in contrast to human mortality—that existed on the lips of men. As C. M. Bowra points out in *The Greek Experience*, "in the thought of glory most Greeks found a consolation for the shadowy doom which awaited them in the grave." Satan of *Paradise Lost* parallels in his behavior the type of Greek hero with whom Milton was familiar from his reading. As Bowra says:

The Humanistic Background

The essence of the heroic outlook is the pursuit of honor through action. The great man is he who, being endowed with superior qualities of body and mind, uses them to the utmost and wins the applause of his fellows because he spares no effort and shirks no risk in his desire to make the most of his gifts and to surpass other men in his exercise of them. His honor is the center of his being, and any affront to it calls for immediate amends. He courts danger gladly because it offers the best opportunity for showing of what stuff he is made. Such a conviction and its system of behavior are built on a man's conception of himself and what he owes to it. And, if it has any further sanctions, they are to be found in what other men like himself think of him. By prowess and renown he gains an enlarged sense of personality and well being. . . .[68]

Satan has some of these characteristics, particularly in his role as a feudal leader (see Chapter IV). But we must not overlook the mock-heroic pattern, running submerged through *Paradise Lost*, by which certain classical values are subordinated to the supernatural ones of Christianity, in which false glory is contrasted with true glory. Milton was deeply aware of the Christian evaluation of "honor through action," of classical glory readapted in this sense. Like "the robber Prometheus" Satan violated the *prima musica*, the cosmic harmony, by ignoring that his own glory had to be in due proportion, in due contribution, to the universal glory of God. As a result of the Fall, the glory of the world has to be held suspect. "Lycidas," in recalling that fame does *not* grow on mortal soil but that the crown of glory truly depends on the "perfect witness of all-judging Jove," parallels the well-known thought of Boethius in *The Consolation of Philosophy*:

Let the wicked rage ever so wildly, the wise man's crown shall never fail or wither, and the wickedness of bad men can never take away from good men the glory which belongs to them.[69]

NOTES

[1] Arnold Stein, *Heroic Knowledge* (Minneapolis, 1957) 27.
[2] *Ibid.*, 33.
[3] *The Christian Doctrine* I, ii, CE, XIV, 31.
[4] *The Christian Doctrine* I, xxx, CE, XVI, 279. Milton observes in *Animadversions* (*Complete Prose*, I, 699): "For certainly, every rule and instrument of necessary knowledge that God hath given us, ought to be so in proportion as may be wielded and managed by the life of man without penning him up from the duties of humane society, and such a rule and instrument of knowledge perfectly is the holy Bible."
[5] *Tetrachordon, Complete Prose*, II, 588.
[6] *The Christian Doctrine* I, xxvi, CE, XVI, 101.
[7] *The Reason of Church Government* II, ii, *Complete Prose*, I, 827.
[8] *The Christian Doctrine* I, xxx, CE, XVI, 281.
[9] "For ask them, or any protestant, which has most authority, the church or the scripture? They will answer, doubtless, that the scripture." *Treatise of Civil Power in Ecclesiastical Causes*, CE, VI, 12.
[10] *The Christian Doctrine* I, xxx, CE, XVI, 265. Milton also observes in the same chapter that "under the Gospel we possess, as it were, a twofold Scripture; one external, which is the written word, and the other internal, which is the Holy Spirit, written in the hearts of believers . . ." (CE, XVI, 273).
[11] *The Christian Doctrine* I, xxx, CE, XVI, 259.
[12] *A Treatise of Civil Power*, CE, VI, 13.
[13] *The Christian Doctrine*, prefatory remarks, I, v, CE, XVI, 177.
[14] *The Christian Doctrine* I, xxx, CE, XVI, 259.
[15] *Likeliest Means to Remove Hirelings*, CE, VI, 75.
[16] *The Christian Doctrine* I, xxx, CE, XVI, 279.
[17] *A Treatise of Civil Power*, CE, VI, 6.
[18] *The Reason of Church Government* II, *Complete Prose*, I, 828.
[19] *Ibid.*
[20] Robert Martin Adams, *Ikon: John Milton and the Modern Critics* (Ithaca, N. Y., 1955) 175.
[21] *The Christian Doctrine* I, xxx, CE, XVI, 283.
[22] Milton is careful in *The Doctrine and Discipline of Divorce* II (*Complete Prose*, II, 295), to stress that God's secret will is just, and consistent with his revealed will: "It is wondered how there can be in God a secret and revealed will; and yet what wonder if there be in man two answerable causes." In *The Christian Doctrine* I, iv (CE, XIV, 109), he denounces the scholastic distinction which gives God a twofold will,

"his revealed will, whereby he prescribes the way in which he desires us to act, and his hidden will, whereby he decrees that we shall never so act: which is much the same as to attribute to the Deity two distinct wills, whereof one is in direct contradiction to the other."

[23] Basil Willey, *The Seventeenth Century Background* (London, 1946) 239.

[24] Emrys Jones, "Stuart Cymbeline," *Essays in Criticism* xi, I (1961) 96.

[25] William Haller, *The Rise of Puritanism* (New York, 1938) 269–270.

[26] *Of Reformation, Complete Prose*, I, 616.

[27] Robert Martin Adams, *Ikon*, 126.

[28] Cf. Chapter I, p. 24 ff.

[29] *A Defence, Complete Prose*, IV, 422.

[30] *The Christian Doctrine* I, x, CE, XV, 115–117.

[31] Denis Saurat, *Milton: Man and Thinker* (London, 1964) 8.

[32] Plato, *The Republic* IV, trans. Benjamin Jowett (New York, Colonial Press, 1901) 129.

[33] *Ibid.*, 134.

[34] Douglas Bush, *Paradise Lost in Our Time* (Ithaca, N. Y., 1945) 37.

[35] *Ibid.*, 39.

[36] In *A Treatise of Civil Power*, Milton states that "it cannot be denied, being the main foundation of our Protestant religion, that we of these ages, having no other divine rule or authority from without us warrantable to one another as a common ground but the holy scripture, and no other within us but the illumination of the Holy Spirit, so interpreting that scripture as warrantable only to ourselves . . ." (CE, VI, 6). In *The Christian Doctrine*, prefatory remarks, I, v (CE, XIV, 179), he speaks of "that spiritual illumination which is common to all."

[37] *Prolusions* VII, *Complete Prose*, I, 293.

[38] Christopher Dawson observes in *Medieval Religion* (New York, 1934) 77–78, that "the theory of the human intelligence is the essential doctrine of Thomism and is the keynote of the Christian Aristotelian synthesis. Hitherto both the Averroist and the Christian Platonist had regarded the spiritual principle of intelligence as something superhuman and divine. It was not in man as part of his personality; it was a power which illuminated his mind from the outside, whether it be regarded with the Christian Platonists as the ray of Divine Light which illuminates the immortal human soul, or whether, as Averroes taught, it was the power of universal intelligence actuating the successive, transitory and mortal minds of men. To St. Thomas, on the other hand, the active intelligence is the very essence of the soul and the root of human responsibility

Ideas in Milton

and liberty. 'For if,' he writes, 'the active intelligence is a substance outside man, the whole of man's activity depends on an extrinsic principle. Man then will not be a free agent but will be acted upon by another, and so he will not be the master of his own acts nor deserve praise or blame; and the whole of moral science and of social science will perish . . . .'"

[39] Arnold Stein, *Heroic Knowledge*, 27.

[40] *The Christian Doctrine* I, iv, CE, XIV, 107.

[41] John Wain, "Strength and Isolation: Pessimistic Notes of a Miltonolater," in *The Living Milton*, ed. Frank Kermode (London, 1960) 2.

[42] Hilaire Belloc, *The Crisis of Civilization* (New York, 1937) 117.

[43] Louis L. Martz, *The Poetry of Meditation: A Study in English Religious Literature of the Seventeenth Century* (New Haven, 1954), 163. Milton was sensitive to the overriding concept of Christian love and makes numerous statements about it, but he was faced with a difficult artistic problem in dramatizing its meaning directly and imagistically in *Paradise Lost*. Douglas Bush observes (*Paradise Lost in Our Time*, 40) that "as a matter of plain fact, Milton does continually stress the prime power of love in God and man; his avowed theme, the assertion of Eternal Providence, means the assertion of eternal love." But the narrative deals with events before the Incarnation, before the great act of divine love that was to inspire so much Christian writing, and the theme of love has to be inferred rather than overt. The relationship between God and himself, as described by Adam in conversation with Raphael (Book VIII), is a little like that of perfect gentlemen, one of whom is a lonely bachelor (Adam), and the other lives in theological self-sufficiency ("for none I know / Second to mee or like, equal much less," VIII, 406–407). It is almost impossible in this situation to image the hunger of the soul for God.

[44] *Likeliest Means to Remove Hirelings*, CE, VI, 95.

[45] For a penetration in depth of the views of St. Bernard, see Etienne Gilson, *The Mystical Theology of Saint Bernard* (New York, 1940).

[46] *Prolusions* VII, *Complete Prose*, I, 292.

[47] Sir Thomas More, *Utopia*, trans. H. S. V. Ogden (New York, 1949) 48.

[48] *Ibid.*, 55.

[49] "That virtue therefore which is but a youngling in the contemplation of evil, and knows not the utmost that vice promises to her followers, and rejects it, is but a blank virtue, not a pure, her whiteness is but an excremental whiteness; which was the reason why our sage and

serious Spenser, whom I dare be known to think a better teacher than Scotus or Aquinas . . ." *Areopagitica, Complete Prose,* II, 515–516.

50 *Romeo and Juliet,* III, iii, 55.

51 Argument prefixed to the October Eclogue, *The Works of Edmund Spenser,* ed. Morris and Hales (London, 1904) 476.

52 Thomas More, *Utopia,* trans. H. S. V. Ogden, 46.

53 *Ibid.,* 47.

54 *The Doctrine and Discipline of Divorce* II, xxii, *Complete Prose,* II, 551.

55 *The Christian Doctrine* I, ii, CE, XIV, 33.

56 Even Spenser had been a little apologetic about breaking with Scholastic method. He remarks in his famous letter to Sir Walter Raleigh, prefaced to *The Faerie Queene,* that "to some, I know, this methode will seeme displeasaunt, which had rather have good discipline delivered plainly in the way of precepte, or sermoned at large, as they use, than thus clowdily enwrapped in Allegorical devices." But fundamentally Spenser was in accord with Renaissance aesthetic, as expressed by Sir Philip Sidney in *The Defense of Poesie* (1595), that the philosopher (that is, the traditional Scholastic one) was so "hard of utterance and so misty to be conceived, that one that hath no other guide but him shall wade in him till he be old, before he shall find sufficient cause to be honest."

57 "Pope compared some of the speeches delivered in heaven to the arguments of a 'school divine.' " Sir Walter Raleigh, *Milton* (New York, 1900) 142.

58 William G. Madsen, "The Ideas of Nature in Milton's Poetry," in *Three Studies in the Renaissance* (New Haven, 1958) 200.

59 Basil Willey, *The Seventeenth Century Background,* 13.

60 Walter Pater, *The Renaissance,* (London, 1913) 176–177.

61 *Nicomachean Ethics,* II, 9, in Aristotle, *Basic Works,* trans. Richard McKeon (New York, 1941) 963.

62 Cf. James Hutton, "Some English Poems in Praise of Music," *English Miscellany* (London, 1951) 1–56.

63 *Prolusions II, Complete Prose,* I, 237.

64 "On the Morning of Christ's Nativity," lines 125–132.

65 Robert Burton, *Anatomy of Melancholy,* Part II, Sect. II, Mem. VI, Sub. III (London, G. Bell, 1937) II, 133.

66 *The Christian Doctrine* I, ii, CE, XIV, 61.

67 *Ibid.,* 33.

68 C. M. Bowra, *The Greek Experience* (New York, 1961) 33.

69 Boethius, *The Consolation of Philosophy* (New York, 1943) 81.

III

The Fall of Man

THE FALL in *Paradise Lost* is not simply that of Adam; *it* is that of Adam falling through and with Eve. In conjunction, rather than separately, they represent heroic man. The aesthetic emphasis, it could easily be argued, is on the fall of Eve, though the theological emphasis remains on Adam.

Eve has been responsible for a certain kind of redemption of her own, for she had redeemed Adam from loneliness. Adam, in describing his own creation and his first encounter with God, touches upon this tension. Adam is deeply aware that he is alone, that all the animals of Paradise have mates but Adam has not. God is pleased with Adam's social instincts and perspicacity and, uniquely in Milton's narrative, actually teases him, asking an intriguing question—in effect, "is God lonely?" On this occasion Milton asks an essentially probing question from which he then veers away—discretion here undoubtedly being the better part of valor:

> What think'st thou then of mee, and this my State,
> Seem I to thee sufficiently possest

The Fall of Man

> Of happiness, or not? who am alone
> From all Eternity, for none I know
> Second to mee or like, equal much less.
> (VIII, 403–407)

Adam does not speculate about what might be a partial argument on behalf of the Trinity, God's isolation in his self-sufficient transcendence. He is absorbed with an impassioned description of the creation of Eve.

Adam and Eve had been duly warned of obedience, free estate, and the enemy near at hand. Trial, Adam argues, will come unsought (IX, 366), and one should not seek temptation. Yet rather ironically he advises Eve:

> Go in thy native innocence, rely
> On what thou hast of virtue. . . .
> (IX, 373–374)

He does not want to prevent Eve from working in the garden by herself, if that is her wish, "for thy stay, not free, absents thee more" (IX, 372). Is Milton in contradiction to the attitude he expresses in *Comus* about unassailable virtue? Or are we to see a difference between the situation of the Lady in *Comus* and that of Eve, in that the Lady was accidentally separated from her protectors while Eve *voluntarily* moves into danger? In what moral terms are we to assess Eve's initiative? Since it leads to a chain of disasters, presumably it was bad in practice. But if Eve had withstood the temptation, would we not have been "tempted" to praise her courage, self-reliance, and initiative in taking the chance that Milton may now condemn?

Milton knows how to create narrative plausibility; he has an eye for the right psychological detail, such as Eve's dream, her working alone in the noonday hour, the appearance and fragrance of the fruit. Her intellectual curiosity, which Satan uses so effectively against her, serves to endear her to us. Adam later, in Book XII, is to look upon the Fall as the seeking of forbidden knowledge by forbidden means (XII, 278) and to see that it was his folly to aspire beyond his fill of knowledge (XII, 558–560). One remarkable innovation, which has not attracted the attention it should in terms of the "new philosophy" of empirical investigation, is the hint which Milton takes from Genesis that the serpent, the subtlest beast of the field, suddenly addresses Eve in human language. The serpent explains that he has acquired this unusual gift of human speech (after Eve expresses surprise at the fact) by eating of the Tree of Knowledge of Good and Evil. Offering stout empirical evidence, he rather convincingly argues that, if he has advanced so rapidly from brute to human communication, heaven only knows how much Eve would advance, starting from a higher level.

Eve at first believes she has acquired a new source of power. She debates within herself whether she should share such power with her mate. But Milton is emphatic in showing the depths of love, though marred after the Fall by egoism and selfishness, both in Eve and Adam. Eve loves Adam too much not to share her supposed strength with him.

When she brings the news to Adam of what she has done, he is utterly shocked. We are told in a very compressed, dramatic image of the consequences of the sin:

> From his slack hand the Garland wreath'd for Eve
> Down dropp'd, and all the faded Roses shed. . . .
> (IX, 891–892)

This is a "conceit," more or less in the metaphysical tradition, involving the idea that the roses had already faded from an awareness of what has occurred. It is tremendously effective as a symbol of the enormity of the sin, its breadth of devastation.

The Fall of Man

Milton now has the problem of reconciling this sense of great shock on the part of Adam with Adam's ultimate succumbing to Eve's point of view. Adam has learned something that the two brothers in *Comus* were too young to know. The principle that virtue can see by her own light to do what virtue would, simply does not hold in Eve's case:

> But confidence then bore thee on, secure
> Either to meet no danger, or to find
> Matter of glorious trial. . . .
> (IX, 1175–1177)

Adam is fully aware of the consequences of the act, and he knows Eve may have to pay the mysterious penalty of death and he may be left without her companionship. At this point Milton creates in Adam a romantic hero not at all suggested in Genesis, a man who loves his wife so dearly he prefers death with her to life without her. This dimension comes from all the love stories of Europe, from the courtly love tradition, from the essential stuff of romance.

So Adam also eats of the tree. The food acts as a kind of intoxicant, as a euphoria-producing drug, and Milton keeps to the traditional idea that the immediate consequence of the Fall is a disorientation of man's natural desires and appetites. The sexual relationship of Adam and Eve loses much of its dignity; it becomes "play" (IX, 1027) and "love's disport" (IX, 1042). This disorientation enters the intellectual and psychological orders as well. Adam and Eve fall into recriminations and quarreling. The great dignity and peace which initially characterized them are lost, and Milton very successfully conveys the pathos of this situation.

Adam raises most of the major problems and doubts that have been voiced at one time or another in regard to the punishment of original sin. "Inexplicable / Thy justice seems" (X, 754–755), Adam says passionately and with pathos. Adam argues, however, that he had accepted the terms of the contract under which he is penalized. Unfortunately, as William Empson has emphasized, the terms of such a contract, involving the transference of the penalty to all of Adam's descendants, is not dramatized or even made clear either in Genesis or in Milton's narrative.[1] Adam himself asks the question which he does not explore:

> . . . Ah, why should all mankind
> For one man's fault thus guiltless be condemn'd,
> If guiltless?
>
> (X, 822–824)

Adam argues that his descendants are bound to act as he has done, because they will be depraved in mind and will:

> . . . But from me what can proceed,
> But all corrupt, both Mind and Will deprav'd,
> Not to do only, but to will the same
> With me?
>
> (X, 824–828)

Milton falls back, at this climactic point, on the Late Augustinian and Calvinistic doctrine of total depravity. Adam's descendants inherit the guilt as well as the natural consequences of Adam's sin.

A mystical or an evolutionary approach would temper this dilemma which, even in the best light, makes God questionable in terms of justice as the human mind sees it. Milton was not acquainted with medieval mystical literature; he did not have any moving mystical concept of the unity of the human race: that the human race is one, that the evil befalling one befalls all, or that the good that happens affects all. Michael in Book XII dismisses into outer darkness the major portion of mankind,

The Fall of Man

apparently without compassion or regret. Christ of the *Paradise Regained*, in spite of Milton's expressed thought to the contrary in *De Doctrina Christiana*, far from dying for all men, for the human race as a unity, obviously has an aristocratic contempt for the disorderly masses:

> For what is glory but the blaze of fame,
> The people's praise, if always praise unmixt?
> And what the people but a herd confus'd,
> A miscellaneous rabble, who extol
> Things vulgar, and well weigh'd, scarce worth the praise?
> (*Paradise Regained* III, 47–51)

The evolutionary approach is more compatible with Milton's whole line of thought. If we are to adhere to the theory of the "paradox of the Fortunate Fall" (the theory that the Fall was eventually the occasion of a greater good coming into being by the fact of the Redemption), some gains, or possibility of gains, must be discernible. One psychological development that Milton, as an artist, stresses in the relationship of Adam and Eve is a transference of attention from ideal and abstract concepts, characteristic of Paradise, to a more complexly personal, even if difficult and frustrating, relationship after the Fall. While one would hesitate to use the word "evolution" in regard to the epic, since this term was to emerge meaningfully at a later stage in intellectual history, there remains a kind of constructive evolution, within the framework of real losses, in the allegory of the Fall as Milton presents it. The possibility is indicated of development toward a full self-consciousness that could be simultaneously harmonized with a full "relating" to the other person. This was ultimately to be established, as some theologians see it, in the Incarnation, where full self-consciousness could be attained without the regression in the Fall (for the Fall in Milton's work develops self-consciousness, but at a great loss)—man in and through Christ could become fully self-conscious ("I am in the Father and the Father in me," John 14:11 ff.) and yet reach out with a full awareness of the other.

Some religious commentators have interpreted the Fall as the subordination of agape (love in the Christian sense of charity and benevolence) to eros (including sexual desire).[2] Certainly this element is present in Milton. Both agape and eros are necessary, and, in a proper relationship, both good. But when eros has become self-conscious, self-regarding in an egoistic sense, we have the problem of that evil which theologians have familiarly termed "concupiscence." Concupiscence is desire but in a regressive sense. It does not fully reach out to the other but is merely exploitive and self-seeking. The problem of a complete fulfillment is how to be fully aware of oneself and at the same time fully aware of the other.

Adam and Eve at the beginning of their relationship are completely happy children. For them to move toward adulthood implies risk as any evolutionary movement does. They are injured, and there are some losses, but there are some gains. In our own experience, the adolescent has to begin to declare his independence from his parents, even at the risk of rejecting important values and making serious mistakes. He has to grow, although it is often painful. Neither life nor wise human beings try to incarcerate him in a state of innocence. The point would seem to be that this stress and strain are necessary to move to a higher level of existence. At first one may fail on this higher level, but, in terms of values, is it not better to fail, at least for a time, on a higher level than to remain forever on a lower level? Many an evolutionist would say yes. If the paradox of the Fortunate Fall means anything, does it not mean that in God's foreknowledge the consequences of the Fall were to lead to a higher stage of development? According to some thinkers (Teilhard de Char-

The Fall of Man

din, for example), man is unique in the animal kingdom in that he is the only being who can use a regression as the basis for a big leap forward. Not that the regression, the Fall, is a good thing in itself, but God, particularly as viewed in terms of evolution, can indeed bring good out of evil.

For Milton, man has no merit in himself in the sight of God. Grace is the bond that gives man meaning. Grace is extended to those who renounce both their *righteous* and unrighteous deeds (*Paradise Lost* III, 292). "Prevenient" grace was extended to Adam and Eve, however not to Satan. Milton's implication is that Satan sinned through knowledge but Adam and Eve, through being deceived. In the case of Satan, then, it would seem that Milton set aside his Platonic concept of the relationship between knowledge and virtue. Satan knew what was not good and deliberately chose it. "Evil be thou my Good" (IV, 110) is a prescription outside of Milton's Platonic world, for Plato optimistically believed that men will always seek the truly good if only they know what it is. However, even Adam and Eve cannot, after the Fall, seek the good merely through their own natures—only through "prevenient grace":

> Thus they in lowliest plight repentant stood
> Praying, for from the Mercy-seat above
> Prevenient Grace descending had remov'd
> The stony from thir hearts, and made new flesh
> Regenerate grow instead. . . .
> (*Paradise Lost* XI, 1–5)

Michael argues that one of the long-range effects of original sin is the loss of "rational liberty," of which Adam and Eve were in possession for a time:

> . . . yet know withal,
> Since thy original lapse, true Liberty

> Is lost, which always with right Reason dwells
> Twinn'd, and from her hath no dividual being:
> Reason in man obscur'd, or not obey'd,
> Immediately inordinate desires
> And upstart Passions catch the Government
> From Reason, and to servitude reduce
> Man till then free.
> (XII, 82–90)

But even after the loss of "rational liberty" the future will be brighter—at least for some. After Michael has outlined the course of the Redemption in Book XII, Adam is deeply impressed and grateful and gives explicit expression to the "*felix culpa*" theme, the paradox of the Fortunate Fall:

> O goodness infinite, goodness immense!
> That all this good of evil shall produce,
> And evil turn to good; more wonderful
> Than that which by creation first brought forth
> Light out of darkness! full of doubt I stand,
> Whether I should repent me now of sin
> By mee done and occasion'd, or rejoice
> Much more, that much good thereof shall spring,
> To God more glory, much more good will to Men
> From God, and over wrath grace shall abound.
> (XII, 469–478)

The Christian life fully lived shall produce a paradise happier by far than the one which was lost:

> . . . then wilt thou not be loath
> To leave this Paradise, but shalt possess
> A paradise within thee, happier far.
> (XII, 585–587)

Some critics have particularly stressed this inward theme in the epic, especially Louis Martz in *The Paradise Within* (1964) and

The Fall of Man

Northrop Frye in *The Return of Eden* (1965). Frye comments that "Milton's source told him that although heaven is a city and a society, the pattern established on earth by God is not social but individual, and not a city but a garden."[3] He maintains that "the theme of externalizing the demonic and the internalizing of the divine runs through every aspect of Milton's writing."[4]

THE HUMAN SITUATION

How does man in his present condition participate in the harmony, in the sense of glory, of which we have previously spoken? According to Milton, only imperfectly and through continued struggle. Man runs both a race of glory and a race of shame. Milton accepts unreservedly St. Paul's metaphor of the Christian life as a race, as an unremitting contest. "I cannot praise a fugitive and cloistered virtue, unexercised and unbreathed, that never sallies out and sees her adversary, but slinks out of the race, where the immortal garland is to be run for, not without dust and heat. Assuredly we bring not innocence into the world, we bring impurity much rather; that which purifies us is trial, and trial is by what is contrary."[5]

Temptation, under these terms, would seem to be an essential element in the Christian life; yet temptation, to be meaningful, can only exist where there is a very real and present danger of failure, of disaster. If virtue implies some kind of predestined status which is simply confirmed by temptation, then temptation is merely a charade. In this respect, we have very different kinds of temptation met by the Lady in *Comus* and by Eve in *Paradise Lost*. Temptation itself suggests a serious tension in a universe seeking harmony, a universe in which evil and temptation are instruments toward assuring glory. There had existed, of course, a long theological tradition which had implicitly reversed the statement in the Lord's prayer, "lead us not into temptation," to mean "lead us, O Lord, into temptation that thereby we may prove our merit." This rather confident attitude toward meeting temptation had been moderated by many theological warnings against "presumption."

Milton in the *Areopagitica* makes the interesting observation that the consequence of the Fall is the learning of what is good through knowing what is evil. The impact of the phrase "that which Adam fell into" should be considered: "It was from out the rind of one apple tasted, that the knowledge of good and evil, as two twins cleaving together, leaped forth into the world. And perhaps this is that doom which Adam fell into of knowing good and evil, that is to say of knowing good by evil."[6]

This would suggest that the loss of innocence is accompanied by a special kind of knowledge. This statement does not preclude knowing through other means: the innocent may also gain in knowledge. But in knowledge of what? We have a semantic problem here, in which the word "knowledge" is largely synonymous with "experience." In bald terms, we might say that "having an idea of" is not the same thing as "knowing something." No philosopher, not even Rousseau, has ever claimed that we are actually living in a completely innocent world. We might be able to imagine such a world, but we do not *know* it. Have we the right to restrict "knowing" to a recognition of something that is verifiable by experience? The dilemma in *Paradise Lost* partly arises from Adam and Eve not really knowing what is evil through experience.

God has decreed the penalty of death for transgressing his prohibition about the fruit of the tree. But Adam lacks any real knowledge about death, either theoretical or experiential. He notes, "So near grows Death to Life, whate'er Death

The Fall of Man

is . . ." (*Paradise Lost* IV, 425). Satan emphasizes forcefully the situation brought about by at most imperfect knowledge:

> Shall that be shut to Man, which to the Beast
> Is open? or will God incense his ire
> For such a petty Trespass, and not praise
> Rather your dauntless virtue, whom the pain
> Of Death denounc't, whatever thing Death be,
> Deterr'd not from achieving what might lead
> To happier life, knowledge of Good and Evil;
> Of good, how just? of evil, if what is evil
> Be real, why not known, since easier shunn'd?
> God therefore cannot hurt ye, and be just;
> Not just, not God. . . .
> (IX, 691–701)

Eve responds to the temptation at least in part because of her ignorance of experience:

> What fear I then, rather what know to fear
> Under this ignorance of Good and Evil,
> Of God or Death, of Law or Penalty?
> (IX, 773–775)

Milton's statement in the *Areopagitica* has another implication. The knowledge of good and evil is that of two twins cleaving together. Would the innocent have any knowledge of good? If so, what kind of knowledge? The acquaintance of Adam and Eve with evil, in spite of the instructions of Raphael, still seems a matter of words; it might be an exaggeration even to call it theoretical knowledge. In a state of innocence would any knowledge have been necessary? One cannot be said to have knowledge of what doesn't in some way exist, and evil would not have existed. Is it not a fact that a great many words denote meaning only through a simultaneous mental association with their opposites? If sickness were unknown in our world, would we have a word for health? If we lived in a world of complete innocence, we would not have a word for "evil"; and if we had no word for evil, why should we need one for good? Actually, in word relationships like sickness-health, good-evil, we are referring to the basic relationships of two ideas, even when we use the words separately. We cannot think of goodness without thinking of evil; we cannot think of health without thinking of sickness. We have some right to suspect that God the Father may have been speaking above the head of Adam in the latter's account (VIII, 317 ff.), for his words had no reference to Adam's experience.

A dilemma practically impossible to overcome, therefore, exists in any attempt to create a vocabulary of innocence in *Paradise Lost*. Adam and Eve are bound to express ideas before the Fall that apparently could only have been germinated through experience after the Fall, or else, as some critics argue, their innocence was never absolute but only relative.

One of Milton's own statements about evil raises a crucial problem of ambiguity:

> Evil into the mind of God or Man
> May come and go, so unapprov'd and leave
> No spot or blame behind.
> (*Paradise Lost* V, 117–119)

How innocent is Milton's God?[7] The statement does not in itself guarantee nonapproval of evil. If God is cast into the role of omniscience as in the tradition of scholasticism, he should be able to foresee every contingency, including that of evil. A theological conundrum remains, for who is to blame God, since by theological definitions he is blameless? Milton's own statement, however, promotes psychological insecurity, for what if God were to *approve* the evil that enters the mind? The assumption, of course, is that God would *know* better than to do such a

The Fall of Man

thing. He should be guided by right reason, for he is right reason himself. Evil entering into the mind of God could not in orthodox terms mean more than that God is aware of the potential for willful deficiency in the universe through the perverted use of freedom. But Milton's context suggests on the surface that God himself might be open to temptation. There is a wide gulf between innocence being aware of the potential of evil, and innocence itself being temptable and open to corruption. Adam presumably had right reason and innocence but managed to fall. Milton does not explain whether God is in a radically different position. One explanation might be that every possible knowledge is open to God but not to Adam.

One critic has observed that "*Genesis*, to which Milton must needs adhere, represents the Fall as due to, or consisting of, the acquisition of that very knowledge, the knowledge of good and evil, by the possession of which alone Milton the humanist believed that man could be truly virtuous."[8] How thoroughly convinced is Milton in referring to the Fall as "that doom which Adam fell into" or "knowledge of good bought dear by knowing ill"? Is he merely subscribing to established theological clichès, while unconsciously beginning to formulate another point of view? While Milton has accepted the theological premise that the Fall is a calamity, it has been argued that it is difficult for him not to consider all knowledge as of value in itself. On the other hand, if knowledge in the *Areopagitica* context is equated merely with knowledge of *experience*, the implication might be different. One can recover from the harmful effects of an experience, but it still might have been better not to have had the experience at all. The point would seem to be that the human being sees in actuality a chain of events that really happen; he can only imagine other possibilities and alternatives. The damage of the Fall is not irreparable; it sets in action a chain of effects that we know; without the Fall another chain of effects would have taken place that we do not know and for which we have no words. But the problem of knowledge is pivotal to any interpretation we may make of *Paradise Lost*, for Adam's degree of knowledge has bearing on the degree of his free will, the degree of his guilt, and on the kind of evil subsequently ensuing.

THE NATURE OF THE FALL

In *Paradise Lost* III, 120-128, God the Father states:

> So without least impulse or shadow of Fate,
> Or aught by me immutably foreseen,
> They trespass, Authors to themselves in all
> Both what they judge and what they choose; for so
> I form'd them free, and free they must remain,
> Till they enthrall themselves: I else must change
> Thir nature, and revoke the high Decree
> Unchangeable, Eternal, which ordain'd
> Thir freedom: they themselves ordain'd thir fall.

Clarence E. Greene offers four possible meanings for the word "freedom" as used here: freedom from external coercion; freedom to obey the undeceived rational faculty; freedom to obey the deceived rational faculty; freedom to disobey the undeceived rational faculty.[9] Logically there ought to be freedom to *disobey* the deceived rational faculty, but Milton gives no evidence of this. Greene argues that Eve's will is free in the sense that she is free to obey the deceived rational faculty; Adam's will is free in the sense that he is free to disobey the undeceived rational faculty. The will that is free in the sense of obeying the undeceived rational faculty is, according to this interpretation, the completely rational will that Milton as a humanist wished to believe in but which his Puritanism and his observation of human nature precluded. Greene holds that the dilemma that

The Fall of Man

Milton encountered was that, as a Platonist, he believed that when a man is compelled to choose one of two evils, no one will choose the greater when he may have the less. Yet Milton had to present Adam doing just this: disobedience to right reason followed by pain and death, rather than obedience followed by immortal loneliness. Northrop Frye suggests that Adam should have divorced Eve,[10] and E. L. Marilla speaks of Adam's "short-sighted altruism."[11] The assumption is that the tenderest love story is not worth all the calamities that followed Adam's assent to Eve's sin and that no one would expect God the Father to change the unchangeable.

For Milton, it has been contended, nothing could be worse than immortal loneliness or ignorant obedience. As a humanist Milton had to remove Adam from Paradise, where ethical development, it is argued, was impossible. Man was driven from the "Eden of the Unconscious" when he began to reason.[12] In the eyes of the humanist, Adam chooses a good without which the Incarnation and Redemption are impossible. Adam really obeys "right reason" after all. But the right reason his will disobeys (the arbitrary will of God) is different from the right reason his will obeys (that of the human mind fully informed with the knowledge of the issues of actual human life).

It could be argued, in contrast to the last point of view, that such an interpretation might more suitably express an idea of original sin in itself rather than Milton's conscious view of it, for it implies that God might have real purposes rather different from his public pronouncements. In *De Doctrina Christiana* I, iv, in dealing with predestination, Milton denies that God has a "two-fold will: his revealed will, whereby he prescribes the way in which he desires us to act, and his hidden will, whereby he decrees that we shall never so act."[13]

Some interpretations of the Fall bypass a number of theological issues by viewing the Genesis narrative as an allegory of man trying to go against the established order of things. Thus E. M. W. Tillyard regards the Fall as a violation of the natural order: "Such disobedience is near to what is now popularly described as the act of disregarding the facts of existence, going against the nature of things, or refusing to come to terms with the conditions of one's environment."[14] E. L. Marilla sees the sin as upsetting the timetable of a divine plan. Man, he argues, was, according to the Renaissance concept, in a status just below that of the angels, and he was originally destined to ascend to their status gradually, through a progressive spiritual refinement. Eve repudiates God's initial plan for the future of mankind, and Adam deliberately acquiesces in Eve's defection. "His sin was precisely that of wilfully sacrificing the universal and ultimate good in the world in the interest of individual and present 'benefits.' "[15] "The sin in the Garden of Eden as Milton depicts this sin was the result of what was generally regarded in Renaissance thought as the source of all human failure on a grand scale—man's misconception of his own nature, and hence, misconception of his basic needs."[16] Adam recovers from a desperate situation by courageously overcoming despair, as expressed by his final resolution to face his own guilt, and by meeting real but inevitably changed conditions. From Basil Willey's point of view, Milton was a Promethean, a Renaissance humanist, faced with the problem of a myth that yearned for innocence and benign coercion.[17] The Fall only went against the nature of things by improving them. Adam could not will what was right until he was capable of sin. The Fall was therefore a necessary state in the evolution of man.

Milton might well have agreed with many varying interpretations of the Fall, for, as he believed, all sins are included in original sin (see Chapter I). Nor would he necessarily disagree

The Fall of Man

with an evolutionary interpretation, for it is the function of Providence, in contrast to Satanic purpose ("out of good still to find means of evil"), out of Satanic evil to "seek to bring forth good" (*Paradise Lost* I, 162 ff.). He would not have agreed that the Fall was a necessary prelude to evolution, but would grant that God could make it serve as the prelude. Milton does not use a stronger word than "seek," since involved in bringing good out of evil is the problem of freedom. Freedom is choice, Milton has said, and to coerce, rather than to persuade, is to destroy freedom.

THE JUSTIFICATION OF PROVIDENCE

To "assert Eternal Providence, / And justify the ways of God to men," even if it could be done in any state of imperfect knowledge, is an enormous assignment and has seemed to quite a few critics inordinately ambitious. Some simply dismiss Milton's argument as irrelevant or unimportant, as in Sir Walter Raleigh's comment that the *Paradise Lost* is a monument to dead ideas.[18] Irene Samuel finds that justification is not the purpose of the poem but "the level at which Milton hopes to deal with his subject, a level consistent with the provident justice of the universe man inhabits."[19] But, assuming that Milton undertakes such an argument, the advocate must never hold back his hand; all the essential evidence must be presented, nothing must be neglected or unanticipated. Such difficulties can, of course, be ignored if "God" is simply regarded as a character in a narrative, but obviously Milton did not intend that the epic be accepted merely on that level. The advocate cannot do his cause justice if he maintains that some of the potential evidence is beyond his ability to understand or is better hidden.

To Milton's credit, he does confront the difficult problems, though he sometimes feels obliged to veer away from a penetration in depth. He is not as evasive as Alexander Pope, who in his *Essay on Man* has a similar overtly stated purpose. Pope cuts the ground from under his theme by ambiguously warning us, in an effort to vindicate the ways of God to man, "presume not God to scan"[20] and by asserting that "in reasoning pride our error lies."[21] Pride apparently is an exception to Pope's own generalization that "whatever is, is right."[22] The latter generalization confuses ontology with the status quo, for if we are to accept the traditional interpretation that evil is the perversion or absence of being, the status quo is often evil, not because of what it contains, but because of what is lacking in it. A slum is evil not because of what is there, but because of deficiency. A slum is good in so far as it is a shelter; it is evil in so far as the shelter is not sufficiently what it should be. The status quo consists not only of what is (or "being"—a thing is good in so far as it is); it also consists, to speak paradoxically, of what isn't. Any inquiry in depth into Pope's thesis can conveniently fall under the category of pride, as Pope defines it. Milton, by comparison, possesses intellectual subtlety and a certain daring honesty.

On the other hand, critics who refuse to take Milton's theological arguments seriously and who examine his epic as a work of art without serious reference to them deserve some sympathy. It can reasonably be asked whether a work of art, particularly an epic, is a suitable medium for this kind of evidential justification. To be effective a work of art must appear to be a completed and unified structure, at least on one definite level. The overtones and challenges to the imagination that a great work of art gives as an incidental bonus need not have any visible unity, for unity can be achieved in various ways—in terms of a logical structure, in terms of a metaphoric structure, in terms of a nar-

The Fall of Man

rative structure. It could readily be argued, of course, that *Paradise Lost* possesses unity on all three levels.

But the logical structure in Milton's epic, for better or worse, is inescapably obtrusive, for in *Paradise Lost* we are dealing with a comparatively rare form of art. We come to *Paradise Lost* with certain unique predispositions. The most convenient analogy is to the medieval play of *Everyman*. Death solemnly commands Everyman to stand still,[23] asking whither is he thus gaily going. Everyman is everyone in the audience as well as the symbolic stage character called Everyman. We are implicated in that play in an unusual way, for we go beyond the process of simple identification normally necessary in the arts. *Everyman* cracks the protective screen of detachment usual in an audience; it hits the spectator in an especially personal, aggressive way. Similarly, in reacting to *Paradise Lost*, how consistently can we regard God the Father, Christ, Satan, Adam simply as "characters" in a work of art? In fact, Miltonic criticism from Dr. Samuel Johnson to William Empson often shows an involvement that has ceased to be specifically aesthetic and instead has become a debate on the issues.

How many of us, on reading Milton, sooner or later find ourselves asking penetrating questions about theology and philosophy? Do we not become intrigued with all the presuppositions of "justifying the ways of God to men"? Milton raises first-rate issues and encourages us to think in a first-rate way. We want to know whether Milton *did* justify God; we want to know the degree to which he succeeded or did not succeed. The *Paradise Lost* is a poem, a work of art. Otherwise we would not be reading it today. However, it is also a theology, an aggressive conclusion about man and his destiny which is bound to invite challenge.

Obviously, a special kind of dilemma is created when a heroic effort is made to synthesize a theological system with a work of art. The logical structure required to justify the ways of God may be deficient or lacking in total unity because of the pressures of form and format that the epic structure itself imposes. One cannot argue as freely and as completely in an epic as in a theological treatise. Nor does the language of metaphor perform the meticulous and narrow job needed for the full subtlety of intellectual justification. Milton cannot escape this difficulty by one of his several approaches to knowledge (for example, that the essence of religious truth is plainness and brightness), for if such approaches were maintained, not only would the justification of God be unnecessary, but the epic itself would have no reason for existence.

Milton is not simply an aesthete, nor is he writing for amusement. He is writing sophisticated religious art and must bear the burdens of such sophistication. While both sophisticated and primitive religious art can be great in their respective ways, their postulates and techniques are quite different. Marc Connelly in *Green Pastures* can present God as a kind of benevolent Negro overseer of a Southern plantation without violence to history or theology, because he also dramatizes a childhood vision, powerful and intuitive, in which the overseer remains very much God. This same artistic method is followed in many medieval illustrations, as in the shepherds bringing their gifts to the Christ child in the *Second Shepherd's Play*. The audience is not asked for intellectual analysis but for the acceptance of initial postulates that are affirmed aesthetically without the need for a rationalizing substratum. To a great extent, Dante, whose intellectual powers cannot be minimized, was a primitive religious artist. Dante applied an accepted body of theology and philosophy to a poignant human context; he is not the author of a

The Fall of Man

De Doctrina Christiana who is questioning what may seem to him certain outmoded theological postulates and who conceivably may feel that the various sects of nonconformist Protestantism need new revelations and a new, more organized theology.

Critics have not been wanting who have questioned the efficacy of *Paradise Lost* as a logical structure. David Daiches, for example, simply states that "Milton overlooked the fact that there is no 'logical' answer to the question of evil existing in a world ruled by a power who is both omnipotent and benevolent."[24] Northrop Frye emphasizes a gulf between the dramatic and conceptual aspects of the poem; the theological situation is sometimes the opposite of the dramatic one; the theological message is not the same as the aesthetic and emotional one. He observes of God the Father that he "keeps on speaking at intervals, and whenever he opens his ambrosial mouth, the sensitive reader shudders. Nowhere else in Milton is the contrast between the conceptual and the dramatic aspects of a situation so grotesque."[25] He adds rather wryly:

> It seems, to sum this up, very strange that the main "argument," in the more limited sense of the doctrinal coherence of the poem, should be so largely entrusted to the one character who is conspicuously no good at argument; and I find that the objections of students and many critics to the poem usually reduce themselves to a single one: Why is everything rational in *Paradise Lost* so profoundly unreasonable?[26]

Louis Martz finds the last two books of the epic, in particular, vitiated by an incomplete synthesis of theological concept and poetic power:

> Milton's plan seems clear: to put Adam through a series of fearful and destructive tableaux, saying the worst that can be said of the world—and then to promise the redemp-

tion of all this at the end of Book XI by displaying the rainbow of God's covenant. Theologically, the design may be said to work; poetically, it is a disaster. For if the reader is expected to grasp the workings of grace against sin, they must somehow be given an adequate imagistic and dramatic presentation, to counter the powerful thrust of the scenes of sin. Milton has done exactly this in Book X, in presenting the recovery of Adam and Eve. Here he fails to present any such organic vision, and instead allows a fissure to develop between the concrete representations of sin and the abstract assertions of Adam's "teacher."[27]

Even if the central part of Milton's canvas is coherent and strong, in an aesthetic endeavor as sweeping as this, certain irritations and frustrations are bound to arise. Art in a sense can never be perfect; it might even be maintained that the greater the sweep and depth of the art, the more it touches on every aspect of human experience, the greater will be the number of minor deficiencies. Only a very limited kind of art can be perfect —but it will not be great.

The justification of Providence will more easily suit a Calvinist reader than anyone else. Michael's words of encouragement are tempered by the thought of the enormous losses to the human race. Michael is rather bland about this, but Adam, to his credit, is about to crack at the thought. In Dante, hell is a symbol of justice, and a Christian, like all men, must support justice. Hell must also be a symbol of freedom—those in hell freely chose to be there; it was the most suitable place for them. In his artistic portrayal of Satan, Milton makes it dramatically clear that Satan is exercising a willed preference. But aesthetically, and quite independent of theological values, we have the impression that the tragedy of the human race is a result of a

The Fall of Man

chain of consequences rather than any willed choice. God the Father himself made an important distinction:

> The first sort by their own suggestion fell,
> Self-tempted, self-deprav'd: Man falls deceiv'd
> By th' other first: Man therefore shall find grace,
> The other none.
>
> *(Paradise Lost* III, 129–132)

Calvinism is, to say the least, unsentimental—and harsh to the outsider. Salvation is very much the prerogative of the in-group. God the Father holds all men guilty of the sin of Adam in his commissioning of Christ as the second Adam:

> ... Be thou in Adam's room
> The Head of all mankind, though Adam's Son.
> As in him perish all men, so in thee
> As from a second root shall be restor'd,
> As many as are restor'd, without thee none.
> His crime makes guilty all his Sons. ...
>
> (III, 285–290)

Many non-Calvinist theologians, although ready to accept the consequences of original sin in the natural order, balk at the idea of *inherited* guilt. But even this harsh doctrine might have been artistically assimilated if the figure of Christ had been made warm and personal.

Christ has the redemptive role in *Paradise Lost,* but it may be questioned whether he is as convincing a portrayal as either Adam or Satan. Involved here is the matter of poetic imagery as well as of characterization. The problem may also be a matter of changing poetic taste. We do not respond to military images with the respectful predispositions of the seventeenth-century reader. God the Father here looks upon his Son primarily as a military figure. To the Son is to go the glory of ending the great war (VI, 701). All are to know his power "in Heaven and Hell above compare" (VI, 704). Instead of the rabbi-like figure, walking the hills of Galilee with his staff and scrip, we have the image of a Christ who is commanded, "My Bow and Thunder, my Almighty Arms / Gird on, and sword upon thy puissant Thigh . . ." (VI, 713–714). The battle between the faithful and rebellious is permitted to remain indecisive so that Christ may come in at the right moment and be awarded the credit for the victory. His image is that of a Roman imperator in a bas-relief on a public monument:

> . . . at his right hand Victory
> Sat Eagle-wing'd. . . .
> (VI, 762–763)

In his right hand, he grasps "ten thousand thunders." As the "effectual might" of the Father (III, 170), he is often cast in the image of a great conqueror leading a public parade of captives as in imperial Rome:

> I through the ample Air in Triumph high
> Shall lead Hell Captive maugre Hell, and show
> The powers of darkness bound. . . .
> (III, 254–256)

The vast majority of Christians, Trinitarians or not, approach the idea of God through the image of Christ. God the Father is an august and remote figure, but the immediate image is that of Christ. Milton lacks any immediately personal note, and the kind of glory that God the Father bestows on the Son does a great deal of violence to our mental associations with the Christ of the gospels. The Christ of the gospels is distinguished by a personality that has plumbed the depth of human tragedy and

The Fall of Man

yet remains human in the warmest and most inclusive terms. He has a dignity that would only be made ridiculous by honors heaped upon it from the outside. Traditionally the Christian has sought contact with the Godhead through the Christ of the gospels, who has suffered many of man's predicaments, including the facts of loneliness and death ("May this chalice pass from me," and "My God, why hast thou forsaken me?"). But Christ as a military figure, as the executive agent of the Father, lacks the human warmth that in the gospels makes communication between the human and divine seem natural and inevitable. Here again the problem of art, the limitation of narrative, enters in. Milton has the enormous task of imagining a Christ before the Incarnation. The problem for many readers is to find sufficient resemblance between this figure, Milton's military figure, and the Christ he knows in the gospels. The theme of glory is an essential one in the epic, as we have discussed previously. The God of *Paradise Lost*, whether Milton succeeds in justifying him or not, is presented as possessing true glory, and all, including his Son, reflect that glory, but sometimes glory is used in a conventionalized military sense even in regard to Christ. On one occasion, he is presented as exulting over defeated enemies, dramatizing open contempt for them:

> . . . Mighty Father, thou thy foes
> Justly hast in derision, and secure
> Laugh'st at thir vain designs and tumults vain,
> Matter to mee of Glory. . . .
> (V, 735–738)

In the justification of Providence, Milton does not easily avoid the impression that the bringing of good out of evil is a kind of Pyrrhic victory. Through the long historical accounts in Books XI and XII, we find Adam expressing the desire that he had not lived to bring about all the consequences Raphael leads him to foresee. Psychologically and emotionally the problem is this: How comfortable is the reader in calmly accepting the great losses to the human race outlined by Raphael? If the religious-minded person concentrates his attention on the redeemed, those who are destined for salvation, and ignores those given to destruction, the result may be one of emotional satisfaction. On the other hand, if the reader has the type of mind which leads him to think and feel about the human race as a whole, the sense of loss is not overcome. Milton could have helped, of course, if he had dramatized more effectively in the last books the possibility of free choice—that some *prefer* to be destroyed. This is a theme which is obviously very difficult to present convincingly, and it does not come through in the comparatively dry historical narrative of the last two books. Even then, the question would still remain, in terms of Milton's theology, to what degree did Adam by his own sin "weigh" the freedom of the will in his descendants in the wrong direction? Nor does Christ as a redeeming figure offer hope to more than a minority.

Milton criticized the fallen angels who "sat on a hill retir'd":

> In thoughts more elevate, and reason'd high
> Of Providence, Foreknowledge, Will, and Fate,
> Fixt Fate, Free will, Foreknowledge absolute,
> And found no end, in wand'ring mazes lost.
> (II, 558–561)

But there is irony in the fact that Milton cannot deal with his subject of justifying Providence without occasionally skirting such "wandr'ing mazes" himself. Primitive religious art can assert, since it does not attempt to bring reverenced mystery before the tribunal of the human intellect, but sophisticated religious art runs into danger when it asserts rather than asks ques-

The Fall of Man

tions. Milton took the plunge of attempting to present a more coherent and rationalized explanation of biblical events.

In the designs of Providence, God gambled on the right use of freedom twice, in the creation of the angels and in the creation of man. Both gambles were only partially successful. Did God foreknow these events? Milton would say yes. Since God, as goodness itself, would choose what is best of all conceivable creations and permutations of creation that he could foresee (presumably he could foresee all), these two creations must have represented the least in loss and destruction; yet these losses were great. It would appear, then, that any experiment in freedom entails big losses. God must then have thought that freedom was worth such a price. Milton stopped short of considering this strong theological argument for the value of freedom in the epic itself, though certainly he was not unaware of the idea. In his *Treatise of Civil Power* (1659), in speaking of "the right of Christian and evangelical liberty," he defends freedom against the asserted consequences of license and confusion: "as if God without them [civil magistrates], when he gave us this liberty, knew not of the worst which these men in their arrogance pretend will follow: yet knowing all their worst, he gave us this liberty as by him judged best."[28]

NOTES

[1] Cf. William Empson, *Milton's God* (New York, 1961) 24 ff.

[2] For a study in depth of eros and agape see M. C. D'Arcy, *The Mind and Heart of Love: Lion and Unicorn, A Study in Eros and Agape* (New York, 1947).

[3] Northrop Frye, *The Return of Eden*, 109.

[4] *Ibid.*

[5] *Areopagitica, Complete Prose*, II, 515.

[6] *Ibid.*, 514.

[7] C. S. Lewis remarks (*A Preference to Paradise Lost*, 83) that our own common sense tells us that we no more become bad by thinking of badness than we become triangular by thinking about triangles. He does not believe that the quoted passage can support the doctrine of latent evil in God. He further adds that "it is not even certain that 'God' means more than 'a god' (for the angels are called *Gods*, with a capital letter, in III, 341)."

[8] Basil Willey, *The Seventeenth Century Background*, 247.

[9] Clarence E. Greene, "The Paradox of the Fall in *Paradise Lost*," *Modern Language Notes* LIII (December, 1938) 557–571.

[10] Northrop Frye, *The Return of Eden*, 65.

[11] E. L. Marilla, *The Central Problem of Paradise Lost: The Fall of Man* (Cambridge, 1953) 13.

[12] Basil Willey, *The Seventeenth Century Background*, 248.

[13] *The Christian Doctrine* I, iv, CE, XIV, 109.

[14] E. M. W. Tillyard, "The Crisis of *Paradise Lost*," *Studies in Milton* (London, 1951) 24.

[15] E. L. Marilla, *The Central Problem of Paradise Lost*, 12.

[16] *Ibid.*, 26.

[17] Cf. Basil Willey, *The Seventeenth Century Background*, 255.

[18] "The *Paradise Lost* is not the less an eternal monument, because it is a monument to dead ideas." Sir Walter Raleigh, *Milton*, 85.

[19] Irene Samuel, *Dante and Milton: The Commedia and Paradise Lost* (Ithaca, N. Y., 1966) 64.

[20] Alexander Pope, *Essay on Man*, Epistle II, lines 1-2.

[21] *Ibid.*, Epistle I, 123.

[22] *Ibid.*, Epistle I, 294.

[23] *Everyman*, 85–86.

[24] David Daiches, *Milton* (London, 1957) 182.

[25] Northrop Frye, *The Return of Eden*, 99.

[26] *Ibid.*, 101.

[27] Louis L. Martz, *The Paradise Within* (New Haven, 1964) 150–151.

[28] *A Treatise of Civil Power*, CE, VI, 39.

IV

The Image of Satan

THE MEANING of good and evil—probably the most evaluative terms in the human vocabulary—must be reexamined by every generation. Though they function reasonably well on a popular level, these words are seldom precise enough or unambiguous enough for intellectual analysis in depth. In the case of an artist who possesses a genius for complexity and for providing many levels of meaning at once, their implications and organization have to be carefully unearthed from interrelated contexts. Milton's overt statements on the subject tell us only part of his meaning; they must be supplemented and modified by imagistic tensions, by characterization, by narrative, even by subconscious drives in so far as these can be predicated. And, in the end, our solution may consist only in a dilemma.

In Milton we do have certain guidelines—in medieval philosophy, in the Socrates of Plato, in Scripture, all of which, however, contain their own share of ambiguity and paradox. A great artist says much more than he consciously plans, and reason, though an indispensable tool, is far from being perfect and serving all contingencies. Experience itself, to which art is intimately related, has a way of blunting the edges of fine intellectual tooling. Moreover, each new age sees the giant symbol that a great work of art is, in terms of its own mental preoccupations and anxieties.

The world of words and concepts is somewhat like a still camera. In our conceptual cameras, we freeze our impressions; their dynamism, their becoming-ness are not adequately recorded. Religious thinkers, as much as they may try to the contrary, tend to suggest God as static rather than dynamic, through the limitations of vocabulary itself, in spite of such words as all-knowing, omnipotent, infinite, and so on. The trouble is that conceptualizations themselves are like still films: We have useful definitions of God, useful descriptive words about him, but they have a limited vitality. They do not reflect dynamic experience; they cannot help us to see God as a mystic does, living personality to living personality, a pillar of cloud by day, a pillar of fire by night, the Logos made flesh.

A common medieval image of deity as a monarch seated upon his throne or the crowned Christ holding a globe with the cross upon it expresses the medieval understanding and respect for kingship. But the concept is static and overformalized. The more primitive forms of medieval art, as in the manuscript illuminations where a St. Joseph may be stoking a hearth fire or the Virgin giving the Christ child a bath, have more power and fluidity. The saints, doctors, virgins, and holy martyrs, assembled before the throne of God, listening to the patron saint (of the donors or of the order who commissioned the painting) who is delivering a commencement speech, do little to suggest the vast creative power, the flexibility, the energy of deity. The trouble with a conceptualized God is that he is set, pigeonholed, tied up with words and definitions. He sits on his throne, all unpol-

The Image of Satan

luted, but he is semantically denied creative movement. He lacks the freedom of the present moment—not to mention the freedom of eternity.

Even Dostoevski in his story of the Grand Inquisitor binds the returning Christ with predetermined concepts; the concept of Christ is so set that he must behave in the same way in fifteenth-century Spain as in first-century Jerusalem. It did not occur to Dostoevski that Christ as God might have behaved quite differently from what he had done previously; that he might have suggested to the cardinal that he was talking too much and should retire to an old man's home. Christ, in Dostoevski's story, would not have been so much out of character as out of *concept*.

In contrast to a good deal of the religious writing that preceded him, Milton's work gives an inescapable impression of increasing dynamism in the presentation of religious values. In this sense he compares favorably with Dante, though his techniques are different. Dante, particularly in the Paradise, achieves dynamism and fluidity by the symbolic acuity of his imagery. His images have the tough and even technical realism of the "radical image" we associate with metaphysical poetry, and this realism often provides the supporting substratum of images of great power and beauty. Dante argues comparatively little; he shows, he visions. Milton more frequently follows the road of intellectualism, of reasoning demonstration. His reasoning is often in support of a more fluid, dynamic religious viewpoint. However, when his thought becomes largely conceptual rather than imagistic and metaphoric, he falls into a trap, for conceptual language imposes its own special kind of static imprisonment.

In this sense, the various critics who have maintained that Satan is the real hero of *Paradise Lost* have some aesthetic justification, even if their viewpoint is theologically misleading. They may have misunderstood Milton's conscious intention and, to a great extent, his performance, but Satan is presented in an imagistic language of dynamism, whereas God the Father and Christ, about whom Milton has some dynamic *ideas*, are largely presented in the static language of concept. In the case of Satan, Milton really "gives" aesthetically; in the case of God the Father and of Christ, Milton reasons too much, and reasoning here is an aesthetic handicap. Hence the psychological effect of the work may create an unresolved tension in respect to its intellectual purpose.

SATAN AS IRONIC HERO

Satan is a complexly ironic creation and in this sense is utterly unique in *Paradise Lost*.

In regard to Satan, critics have been repeatedly sensitive to the paradox of the apparently good qualities of an evil being. Some clarification is necessary. The traditional medieval view held that a thing is good in so far as it is—that is to say, ontology (nature, in this sense) is good. Satan is good in so far as he is perceptive, courageous, exercising leadership. Evil, in this view, results from deficiency, from the perversion of a being from its end. Satan is evil in that he uses perception, courage, leadership to the wrong ends. Evil does not possess being; it has no body; it cannot be located in itself, in isolation. St. Augustine in the *Confessions* explains rather dramatically the intellectual difficulty he had in moving from a Manichean position on this problem to the one that was most commonly held by Christian scholars. It took him many years to see evil otherwise than as being, a body, a power.[1]

Medieval philosophy was rather Socratic. It assumed that no man seeks evil (deficiency, perversion) for its own sake; but man may seek a "mistaken" good. A robber seeks to steal a purse.

The Image of Satan

The purse is an ontological good. It still remains an ontological good when it comes into the robber's possession. But the medieval system also stressed a hierarchy of goods: The lower value or good has to be guaranteed by a proper relationship to a higher value or higher good. The robber has violated an ethical good, a value higher than an ontological good represented by the purse; he has violated the good that makes justice and charity possible among men, that makes social life possible. We could conceivably possess many ontological goods and miss those goods that make us truly men. In this sense, there would be no contradiction between the possession of all sorts of good qualities (as in Milton's Satan) and an abysmal failure in relationship to higher values. The "evil" person (Satan) seeks goods (otherwise he would not be a person), but he does not seek the good (God) that guarantees the order of goods.

In the presentation of Satan, Milton is dealing with a special difficulty. He is not presenting a human intelligence but an angelic one—a being the nature of which is almost impossible for the human mind to grasp. Although Milton simplifies the matter by making spiritual intelligences more highly refined versions of human intelligences, he is still left with the question of whether a more highly refined intelligence is any more likely to seek evil for its own sake than any human being. In fact, the difficulty becomes greater, for if Socrates is right in assuming that the pursuit of evil is the result of ignorance, the angelic intelligence, because of its higher capacities, should move even more strongly in the opposite direction. But when Satan says, "Evil be thou my Good," he is, in effect, saying "Deficiency, perversion, be thou my good." Satan's statement, though intensely dramatic in its context (IV, 111), is no credit to any intelligence, angelic or otherwise. It almost justifies C. S. Lewis' observation, "What we see in Satan is the horrible co-existence of a subtle and incessant intellectual activity with an incapacity to understand anything."[2]

A partial explanation can be offered in terms of malice, a perversion of the will which is so intense it can override the basic and insistent demands of the intelligence. While the statement, "Evil be thou my Good," makes nonsense on the surface, it has symbolic meaning as an expression of Satan's act of the will in rejecting the cosmic hierarchy of values. It reflects a massive determination of the will to reject anything that stands above the self. Satan wills complete transcendence and, in doing so, creates an illusory world which he accepts as reality. Satan is not an intellectual responding in a reflective way to the emanations of reality; he has a will that is going to make his own world, including a "Hell of Heav'n" (I, 255), for the mind is its own place—that is, it is committed to complete transcendence.

Satan cannot achieve this transcendence, first of all because it is contrary to the nature of things. But—and this is particularly ironic—Satan's infinite projection of his ego, if this were possible, is completely compromised by hatred. His hatred makes him psychologically dependent upon what he hates, and his hatred of what he hates is made the greater by his dependence on it. Throughout the epic Milton skillfully dramatizes this dependence among the devils—they have a derivative existence; even the hatred that gives them their energy derives from the reality they are blindly bent on rejecting.

SATAN'S SEARCH FOR GLORY

The theme of glory in *Paradise Lost* helps aesthetically to relegate one dilemma of knowledge—how an angelic intelligence can be so unintelligent—to the background and serves to make Satan a more ironic character than ever. He who "cloth'd with

The Image of Satan

transcendent brightness didst outshine / Myriads though bright" (I, 86–87) madly seeks for what he does not seem to realize he had already possessed.

Milton everywhere emphasizes the medieval irony in regard to Satan that sin perverts the judgment and a perverted judgment leads to more sin with an increasing degeneration of the intelligence. Faustus, we remember in Marlowe's play, after signing a very real compact with Mephistopheles, argues that Hell's a fable, and his superficiality makes Mephistopheles tremble. The playwright is not indicating Faustus' new-won freedom from medieval superstition; the dramatic context reveals Faustus' increasing loss of contact with reality. He is becoming less intelligent at the very moment he thinks he is more intelligent. This is Milton's method in the presentation of Satan.

Satan initially lays stress on the "unconquerable will" (I, 106) —"That Glory never shall his wrath or might / Extort from me." True glory rises from the continuing creative action of goodness. Satan is aware of this on one disjointed level of his mind, for he uses this principle in his attempted seduction of Eve in her dream—"good, the more / Communicated, more abundant grows" (V, 72). Satan is bent on misunderstanding the true nature of glory, which is goodness communicated, bestowing a blessing on him who gives as well as him who receives. What is given, as Dante once indicated in one of his images, is returned as in an intensifying mirror;[3] light is multiplied and remultiplies in mutually creative communication. Satan is highly competitive ("aspiring / To set himself in Glory above his Peers," I, 38–39), not concerning the essence of glory, but concerning its appearance—and appearance without essence is simply counterfeit. In Book III of *Paradise Regained* we have a full exploration in explicit terms of Milton's theme of glory, which also underlies so much of *Paradise Lost*. Satan who "insatiable of glory had lost all" (*Paradise Regained* III, 148) contended in another context that the Father imposes the contribution of his glory to be paid by all, willing or unwilling (*Paradise Regained* III, 114). Christ replies to this by asserting that God created primarily out of a desire to communicate goodness and that glory was a secondary effect. This is an important commentary, nowhere else stated so explicitly in Milton:

> To whom our Savior fervently replied.
> And reason; since his word all things produc'd,
> Though chiefly not for glory as prime end,
> But to show forth his goodness, and impart
> His good communicable to every soul
> Freely; of whom what could he less expect
> Than glory and benediction, that is thanks. . . .
> (*Paradise Regained* III, 121–127)

As Arthur O. Lovejoy has pointed out in *The Great Chain of Being*, one of the Greek ideas about deity is that God is the source of creative goodness. It is the very nature of the good to be creative, outgoing, generous, giving of itself. The image frequently used to express this concept is that of a reservoir, always flowing, yet always filled. An alternative Greek view of deity is that of an absolute self-sufficiency. Lovejoy, perhaps through not examining Milton widely enough, believes Milton is preoccupied by the idea of God conceived as self-sufficient transcendence (which, incidentally, was the illusory dream of Satan), rather than the idea of God conceived as the plenitude of goodness. He states with regard to Milton that "there appeared to be in the nature of things not only no reason why any world of imperfect creatures should exist, but every reason why it should not exist," and that a "self-absorbed and unproductive God would be not less, but, if possible, more divine, and that there is no necessity, and, indeed, no reason for the existence of any creature."[4] The basis for Lovejoy's inferences consists in the following passages from *Paradise Lost*:

> And put not forth my goodness, which is free
> To act or not, Necessity and Chance
> Approach not mee, and what I will is Fate.
> (VII, 171–173)

> Thou in thyself are perfet, and in thee
> Is no deficience found; not so is Man. . . .
> (VIII, 415–416)

> Thou in thy secrecy although alone,
> Best with thyself accompanied, seek'st not
> Social communication. . . .
> (VIII, 427–429)

Obviously, in Christianity two traditions persisted: the concept of God as a self-sufficient spirit who alone exists of himself and is infinite in all perfections and the concept of the Incarnation—in which the Logos was made flesh, in which God so loved man that he sacrificed his only begotten Son. The theological problem was to bridge the gap between God's absolute freedom from dependence upon any creature and his sustaining love for his creation. Milton states both doctrines, depending upon context, but since the narrative deals with the creation, the emphasis is on the plenitude of goodness. Ironically, even Satan caught the idea, though his own ambition is to achieve the more sterile aim.

Satan's blind drive toward the impossible, toward a false glory, makes him incapable of seeing a true state of things—his decisive defeat by God, which Satan chooses to attribute to chance or duplicity or new weapons. And while pursuing his mirage of glory, Satan has lost the true glory—the magnanimity which is its essential ingredient and which was derived from a proper relationship to God. Satan and his lieutenants think of attacking heaven's "battlements," belittling it into a fortress state, and of repossessing their "native seat." Heaven has degenerated for them into a mere place, a geographical area suitable for military attack and capture. It is no longer heaven in the sense of a personal and creative relationship between God and his creatures. Heaven is not a place, but a personal relationship, but Satan wants heaven with God out of it; he wants a house but not a home; he wants the accidental features of heaven while throwing away its essence.

As Satan constantly abnegates his capacity for intelligence, he also warps his practical judgment; his tactics become as bad as his strategy. As his real powers decline, he becomes more arrogant and more cocksure. He traps himself in moves that are also *unconsciously* ironic. He offers to venture alone to the new world, because this is the role of leader, who must bear the greatest burden of danger and suffering. While all the leading devils exercised the right of free speech in the giant committee meeting in Book II, Satan had been in control of the destination and outcome of the meeting from the very beginning:

> . . . Thus Beelzebub
> Pleaded his devilish Counsel, first devis'd
> By Satan, and in part propos'd. . . .
> (II, 378–380)

Beelzebub acted as Satan's effective floor manager at the convention. After the plan had passed to search out the new world of man, Satan pointed out all the horrific dangers of the trip. Volunteers did come forward at Beelzebub's request. Satan alone was found sufficient (II, 404) to undertake the task. It is doubtful that Milton meant us to believe that *Satan believed* all that he said. If Satan had believed all he said about the journey, he might not have undertaken it. The irony lies in the fact that the

The Image of Satan

deceiver, using words for psychological propaganda ("this enterprise / None shall partake with me," II, 465–466), while he does not know it, is actually telling the truth. And the other devils, not allowed to share this image of glory, after their heated speeches on military and political strategy must stand by and amuse themselves with athletics, music and philosophical seminars.

Having lost the sense of true glory, Satan has become compulsive, or as we would say today, neurotic, in the pursuit of the false glory. He has believed his own propaganda; he has hypnotized himself with talk about his unconquerable will, his mind not to be changed by place or time, his invincible spirit. As a psychoanalyst has observed, all drives for glory (the false glory) aim at the absolute, the unlimited, the infinite.

> Nothing short of absolute mastery has any appeal for the neurotic possessed with the drive for glory. . . . The neurotic loses in the process his interest in truth . . . a loss that among others accounts for his difficulty in distinguishing between genuine feelings, beliefs, strivings and their artificial equivalents (unconscious pretenses). The emphasis shifts from being to appearing.
>
> . . . .
>
> And lastly, he must develop a system of private values . . . which determines what to like and accept in himself, what to be proud of. But this system of values must by necessity also determine what to reject, to abhor, to be ashamed of, to despise, to hate. It cannot do one without the other. Pride and self hate belong inseparably together; they are two expressions of the one process.[5]

There has been an increasing sensitivity in modern criticism to the possible ironic uses in Milton even of rhetorical imagery. He has rejected the style of joust and tournament as unsuitable to his main theme but has relegated to a lesser level the style suitable to Satan, as a haughty Achilles or crafty Ulysses—in the words of Northrop Frye, "the knight-errant who achieves the perilous quest of chaos."[6] In this connection, the feudal image of Satan as a military leader has its undercurrent of imagistic irony.

A basic theme of the history play as presented on the Elizabethan stage was the proper relationship of the vassal to his overlords, and it often involved the problem of *who* technically and legally was the feudal superior. Satan has such an argument with Abdiel in Book V.

In his role of a medieval military chief Satan argues against the acceptance of Christ, in the medieval terms of first among equals customary in conflicts of barons with the king.[7] The building of Pandemonium in Book II is reminiscent of many medieval conventions. Military and court service was a personal obligation incumbent on all vassals. When the lord wished to make a show of importance, he summoned his vassals to the court. They assembled to settle disputes and give advice. The efficient execution of the feudal "fief" was of mutual concern, and it was expected that the lord would seek the advice of his vassals before making important decisions, especially in any enterprise (particularly war) in which he would need aid. The debate at the beginning of Book II mirrors a feudal council. The successful baron, in this case Satan, respects or appears to respect the rights of each vassal, handling each subordinate tactfully, and there is a great deal of camaraderie and plain speaking. Beelzebub as second in command has functions which are like those of a medieval "seneschal," who is the chief administrative officer of the feudal household and fief.

It is particularly in the military and psychological characteristics of Satan that the feudal tradition is asserted. One of the great medieval principles was that of "noblesse oblige." Adam, for example, in respect to Eve, had the greater gift—therefore, the greater responsibility. In return for special privileges the individual must undergo special risks, and Satan himself makes an exposition of this doctrine:

> ... Wherefore do I assume
> These Royalties, and not refuse to Reign,
> Refusing to accept as great a share
> Of hazard as of honor, due alike
> To him who Reigns, and so much to him due
> Of hazard more, as he above the rest
> High honor'd sits?
>
> (II, 450-457)

The medieval nobleman owed his social prominence over the peasantry to his special role of warrior, and he attached the foremost importance to the virtues of the military life. He regarded honor as the highest achievement open to men. Honor, in effect, meant the public recognition of qualities appropriate to the warrior: readiness to do battle whenever challenged, skill in the use of arms, courage, faithfulness to a trust. Satan constantly exhibits these characteristics. He acts in the role of commander as he advances with haughty stride and derisive words to do battle or when he reviews his assembled troops. As one critic says of Satan, "there is only one figure in *Paradise Lost* whose strength is shown through conflict and endurance."[8] Aesthetically, these associations of feudalism and chivalry do a great deal to enhance the surface impressiveness of the figure of Satan in the epic, but it is also not without a subterranean ironic overtone that this whole order of things was out of date, as lost in the web of time as Achilles or Ulysses in contrast to what Milton considered the ever-present reality of the Christian drama.

THE CONSISTENCY OF SATAN'S CHARACTERIZATION

It may very well be that the very nature of the narrative in *Paradise Lost* as a work of art precludes the presentation of a completely coherent synthesis of all the elements symbolized in Satan. Satan's artistic function, as distinct from any theological one, is to be a good villain (good aesthetically, of course) who sets up the terms of a conflict. The epic is an art of conflict and the artistic focus must fall initially on the instigator of crisis. This does not mean that the instigator wins our emotional sympathy, but it does mean that, for a considerable time at least, he must be the center of interest. We have a parallel situation in Shakespeare's *Othello*, where the dramatic initiative lies with Iago, although as Othello reacts he comes to the center of the stage. There is a similar aesthetic relationship between Satan and Adam. Theologically speaking, attention should focus on God the Father, or the Christ who reflects the Father's glory, rather than Adam, especially if the basic theme is to justify the ways of God to men. But the identification of the audience lies rather with Adam, who, after all, represents the destiny of the human race in *human* terms.

We witness different aspects of Satan according to different projections of him at various climactic points in the narrative. He offers a changing and dynamic image rather than a constantly explicable character. For example, Satan experiences on the sight of Eve a reaction that the Beatific Vision itself could not induce. It is but momentary, and it is hard to know whether Milton simply wanted to indicate something about the attractiveness of Eve in poetic hyperbole or whether he was delivering some sort of dramatic message about Satan. If we were to turn customary terminology upside-down, we might call Satan's hesitation to injure Eve a kind of reversed "tragic flaw," an inclination to follow goodness in the midst of a concerted program of evil:

The Image of Satan

> That space the Evil one abstracted stood
> From his own evil, and for the time remain'd
> Stupidly good, of enmity disarm'd. . . .
> (IX, 463–465)

Obviously, Milton wanted to show Adam's degeneration in stages. Satan, this "less than Arch-Angel ruin'd" whose form had yet not lost "all her original brightness" (I, 590–593), exercises an ironic humanism of his own; he is indeed going to be a Lucifer, a light-bringer of knowledge:

> . . . and do they only stand
> By Ignorance, is that thir happy state,
> The proof of thir obedience and thir faith?
> O fair foundation laid whereon to build
> Thir ruin! Hence I will excite thir minds
> With more desire to know. . . .
> (IV, 518–523)

In the presentation of Satan, Milton is also beset by a technical problem that had plagued Elizabethan art forms. When the classical chorus had been dispensed with, there was, at least in the drama, no ready means of communicating the personal commentary of the author. Frequently, as in Shakespeare's Iago, the villain—though the least psychologically fitted for it—communicates an unsuitable sensitivity to the beauty of virtue. It is Iago who speaks of Othello's free and open nature, of Desdemona's innocence. Herein the villain really doubles as chorus. While Milton as an epic poet can make his own detached commentary, he also employs the technique of the villain-chorus. Satan, for example, goes so far as to admire Adam and Eve because of their "Divine resemblance" (IV, 364), something which, in strict character, he should hate.

An art form not only imposes restrictions on the artist but

also sets up certain directions, certain emphases, that are unavoidable. At all times the artistic form of a narrative itself imposes strains on Milton's theology. For example, if God is all-powerful, he cannot properly be the subject of a narrative conflict. Such a conflict would be too unequal to create suspense. The best the artist can do is to suspend temporarily theological principle and create an atmosphere which conveys the illusion that God is not all-powerful. In the opening two books of *Paradise Lost*, Milton achieves at least partial success by presenting the devils as uncertain about the exact powers both of themselves and of God; they are, in a sense, experimenting to find out. As one critic has stated, *Paradise Lost* "is dramatically real in proportion as you assent to the illusion of equality which the poem communicates."[9]

As regards the tragic impact of the narrative, Milton experiences a special difficulty that was unknown to the Greek or Renaissance art of tragedy. Tragedy would not be tragedy if it were not a painful mystery, but even in the starkest works, such as *Oedipus the King* or *Hamlet*, the spectator can always hope that some balance wheel outside his immediate human experience might set things right on some unknown level or in some world beyond the grave. Fate and the gods influence, and even afflict, men. But in *Paradise Lost* God himself, incorporating fate, directly confronts Satan and Adam. There is no escape, imaginary or real, from the finality of omnipotence in action. The kind of ambiguity immemorially connected with the tragic is removed. Decisions are final, here and hereafter, at some cost in the excitements of speculation, suspense, and wonder.

The artist deals with the mysteries of destiny, death, and justice on a rather different plane from that of the theologian whose statements tend to have a legal patness and sound considerably less human than he intends. The artist has an array of

The Image of Satan

symbols that conveys the concrete complexity of mortal life, a complexity which never quite squares with the orderly procession of even a subtle theology—not to mention a more simplified Calvinistic one. The unknown is one of the important dimensions of tragedy and is deeply causative of the emotions tragedy is classically designed to arouse: pity and fear. The more emphatically theological Milton is, the more he has to reduce the dimensions of the unknown. In view of this problem, it is amazing how little of the tragic atmosphere Milton has sacrificed.

While it is the function of theology to search for answers to the eternal questions, art seems to reach its most mature levels when it *asks* questions in a vividly delineated context. Milton's artistic problem arises from the fact that when he proceeds theologically, he seems to make God (as an aesthetic character) know more (though not with artistic plausibility) than *any man* (as an artist) *really* is assured that God knows. God's knowledge might contain many surprises unanticipated by Milton. Theologically he offers too many answers when as an artist he should be intensifying his questions.

THE CRITICS AND THE IMAGE OF SATAN

Romantic criticism, perhaps best summarized in William Blake's remark in *The Marriage of Heaven and Hell* that Milton was of the devil's own party without knowing it, significantly contributed to the misunderstanding of *Paradise Lost*. Romanticism had its own complexities, its own congeries of ideas and internal reactions, and it failed to be sensitive to the complexities of Christian tradition. The sympathy of the Romantics toward Milton's Satan was due, in large measure, to their absorption with transcendence. They completely missed Milton's ironic commentary on it. Christian transcendence also insisted on the acceptance of certain specific limitations. In Christian thought perfectibility is unlimited, in a vertical sense, in the direction of charity and of a mystical union with God, but it is limited horizontally by the nature of created being itself. Christianity can more easily adjust to classical tradition than to Romanticism, for it also stresses, as does classicism, bounds and controls, whereas Romanticism yearns for the unlimited. Classicism possesses a certain humility that is lacking in the Romantic ethos, even when the latter is most self-flagellatory, for classicism subjects itself to powers it recognizes as outside of itself. In another sense, of course, Christianity is open-ended, fluid, dynamic, always seeking an ever higher and receding perfection, placing no limit on virtue, love and charity.

In its extreme form, Romanticism could see Satan as a great Romantic hero. Byron, for example, like Milton's Satan, is committed to the "eternal spirit of the chainless mind."[10] (A classicist would ask whether the mind could function at all without some pretty tough cables linking it to reality.) In this intense subjectivity, moral values disappear, as Byron himself indicates (in lines ironically echoing words Milton put into the mouth of Satan):

> The mind which is immortal makes itself
> Requital for its good or evil thoughts.[11]

Romantic man frequently becomes isolated, self-subsistent, noncommitted to society (unless engaged in overthrowing it), and all problems wither away, including that of evil. Reality is nothing in itself; it is merely something to be molded by the ego.

Obviously a doctrine of transcendence and subjectivity has to meet the difficult problem of what to do with experience. Many of the Romanticists were intense activists. In opposition to the gospel statement that in the beginning was the Word, or Logos,

The Image of Satan

Goethe's Faust says that in the beginning was the Act. Faust hopes to escape the supposed prison house of Christian doctrine and Christian law by a life of pursuit, where everything is worth pursuing and nothing seems to bring satisfaction except this endless destiny of pursuit itself. Byron went so far as to say that "the great object of life was sensation—to feel that we exist, even though in pain."[12] Satan is not content to enjoy his invincible mind (I, 140) but must go on a busy and destructive rampage. Even Marlowe's Faustus, who regretted that he was "still but Faustus and a man,"[13] had to transcend himself by all sorts of activity characterized by a cosmic triviality. Both Goethe and Marlowe offer a rather ironic commentary on the search for identity through unlimited extension.

Satan's rebelliousness, his seeking of transcendence, his capacity for action, particularly unconventional action, endeared him to certain types of Romantic minds. Nor did Milton create sufficiently powerful poetic images in God the Father or Christ to modify the impression the Romantics were seeking. In his *Defence of Poetry*, Shelley stated that "Milton's devil as a moral being is as far superior to his God, as one who perseveres to some purpose which he has conceived to be excellent, in spite of adversity and torture, is to one who in the cold security of undoubted triumph inflicts the most terrible revenge upon his enemy, not from any mistaken notion of inducing him to repent of any perseverance in emnity, but with the alleged design of exasperating him to new torments." William Empson in our own time has written with acerbic indignation that Milton nailed his conscience to a Bronze Age literature, and that this situation must have unconsciously appalled him.[14]

If Milton's portrait of God does not come through with sufficient inspiration, it still does not follow that Milton regarded Satan in a heroic light, rather than in a mock-heroic or satiric light. An artist projects something of himself into all his characters; this is the way of "empathy," of the creative imagination, but it does not necessarily follow that the artist wants moral approval for such a projection. Moral approval or rejection lies in the reason and the will rather than in the emotions. There can also be degrees of involvement with any situation which includes moral problems. Sir Guyon in destroying the Bower of Bliss in Book II of *The Faerie Queene* understands the charm and enticement of this immoral place, and in that sense we regret its destruction. But Spenser made a solid case for such destruction while recognizing, as an artist and as a man, its powerful seductiveness. Milton would seem to be less emotionally involved with his creation of Satan than Spenser, through Sir Guyon, with the Bower of Bliss. It is a tribute to Milton as an artist that Satan is given the characteristics that make him plausible as the leader of a great insurrection. But this does not mean approval on other levels. Our emotional reaction is supposed to be, as in the case of the Bower of Bliss, one of some emotional regret yielding to the stronger imperative of the reason and the will—Milton's "right reason." Milton is also as devoted to the idea of freedom (though in a different sense) as any Romantic, but not necessarily as manifested in the activities of Satan. Even in his bitterest attacks on bishops, Milton supports what he thinks is legitimate authority; his question always remains, what is legitimate authority? Satan's opposition to God, for example, and Milton's opposition to Charles I are on entirely different levels. The maintenance of justice and right could always be depended upon in the case of God, but not in that of man.

The cult of Satanic heroism has been more or less dissipated in modern criticism. The main interest has centered on the internal consistency of the character. Thus A. J. A. Waldock argues

The Image of Satan

that the changes in Satan's character do not generate themselves from within; his character "does not degenerate; it is degraded."[15] Louis Martz maintains, "There is no problem of degrading Satan. He has from the beginning represented the subtle, pervasive evil that walks and seeps through all the vivid imagery of the first two books, culminating in the vicious allegory of Satan, Sin, and Death, the trinity of evil." He goes on to say that "he has never possessed reality; what reality he has comes from the world of men. So now the symbol of Satan, having served its purposes, can be discarded with contempt."[16] Robert Martin Adams maintains that Satan, on stage, does not develop consistently in any single particular direction. "After being a toad and a schemer in the middle of Book IV, he is heroic 'like Teneriffe or Atlas unremoved' at the end; at one point he is the spokesman for a diseased and strikingly human conscience, then again he is personified evil; at one point he is an audacious solitary adventurer, at another a jocosely complimentary sophist. He is, at any given juncture, whatever it suits man's story to have him, because he is making no new discovery, suffering no new loss, adventuring no new hope."[17] Allan H. Gilbert argues, "So far as this Satan standing for the universal power of evil, he is not to be reconciled with the villain of the garden tragedy. A critic cannot arrive at a unified characterization of the Adversary."[18] Then there is the seventeenth-century reader view; R. J. Werblowsky remarks, "The seventeenth century reader, under the influence of his spiritual climate, really saw the Satan Milton 'intended' to write, sharing Milton's own ignorance as to what he had actually written."[19]

Examples could be multiplied. An ambiguity implicit in all criticism is the degree of closeness in relationship of a character in an artistic construction (to which we react more or less quickly and spontaneously) to nominally the same character as seen in an interpretative and critical reconstruction of a scholar. The critic generally feels obliged to supply, if possible, the logical and other connections in his interpretations, which the artist, in his speed of movement, can happily omit. The Elmer Edgar Stoll thesis about a Shakespearean play (that inconsistencies unnoticed by an audience witnessing the actual production of a play should also be disregarded by the critic in study)[20] can be applied only with difficulty to a theological epic, which invites slow reading and minute analysis. In *Paradise Lost*, in addition to the possible divergence between a character operative in a work of art and the one operative on a critic's pages, we have the actual divergence between Milton's theological thought and the narrative line that the epic art itself imposes.

NOTES

[1] "When I desired to think of my God, I could not think of Him save as a bodily magnitude—for it seemed to me that what was not was nothing at all: this indeed was the principal and practically the sole cause of my inevitable error. Because of this I thought that the substance of evil was in some sense similar, and had its own hideous and formless bulk, either gross which they called earth, or thin and tenuous like the air: for they imagine it to be some malignant mind creeping over the earth. And because such poor piety as I had constrained me to hold that the good God could not have created my nature evil, I supposed that there were two opposing powers, each infinite, yet the evil one lesser and the good one greater; and from this abominable foundation other sacrilegious notions followed." *The Confessions of St. Augustine*, trans. F. J. Sheed (New York, 1943) 97.

[2] C. S. Lewis, *A Preface to Paradise Lost* (London, 1942), 112.

[3] "And the greater the number who comprehend / and love each other, the more love there is, / since each gives to another like a mirror." "Purgatory," XV, 73, *Divine Comedy*, trans. H. R. Huse (New York, 1963) 239.

[4] A. O. Lovejoy, *The Great Chain of Being* (Cambridge, 1936) 160–161.

The Image of Satan

[5] Karen Horney, *Neurosis and Human Growth: The Struggle Toward Self-Realization* (New York, 1950) pp. 34–35, 38, 109.

[6] Northrop Frye (ed.), *Paradise Lost and Selected Poetry and Prose* (New York, 1951) xix.

[7] Maurice Kelley in *This Great Argument* (Gloucester, 1962) 94 ff., makes a detailed analysis of the meaning of the passage: "This day I have begot whom I declare / My onely Son" (*Paradise Lost* V, 603–604), in regard to the umbrage Satan took with respect to it and in regard to its place as a motivating pattern in the artistic construction of the work.

[8] E. M. W. Tillyard, *Milton* (London, 1949) 278.

[9] B. Rajan, *Paradise Lost and the Seventeenth Century Reader* (London, 1947) 96.

[10] Byron, "Sonnet on Chillon" (1816) line 1.

[11] Byron, *Manfred* III, iv, 129–130.

[12] Letter of September 6, 1813, *Byron: A Self-Portrait*, ed. Peter Quennell (New York, 1950) I, 173.

[13] Christopher Marlowe, *The Tragical History of Doctor Faustus* I, i, 23.

[14] William Empson, *Milton's God*, 199.

[15] A. J. A. Waldock, *Paradise Lost and Its Critics* (Gloucester, 1959) 83. B. Rajan, like Waldock, seems to think that Satan missed his opportunity for tragedy. Rajan argues that Satan is heroic in Hell, and melodramatic in Paradise (cf. *Paradise Lost and the Seventeenth Century Reader*, 100–108).

[16] Louis L. Martz, *The Paradise Within*, 137–138.

[17] Robert Martin Adams, *Ikon*, 43–44.

[18] Allan H. Gilbert, *On the Composition of Paradise Lost* (Chapel Hill, 1957) 56.

[19] R. J. Werblowsky, *Lucifer and Prometheus: A Study of Milton's Satan* (London, 1952) 26.

[20] Elmer Edgar Stoll, *Art and Artifice in Shakespeare: A Study in Dramatic Contrast and Illusion* (New York, 1962).

V

Ideas in the Poems

THE COMPANION PIECES

WE MAY speak of *the* theme of "L'Allegro" and of "Il Penseroso" because basically these two poems constitute one work of art. They were created in the Renaissance tradition of "companion" pieces (like matching vases on a mantelpiece). In modern idiom, we would consider them one artistic statement in the mode of "thematic contrast," where two contrasting motifs are juxtaposed to illuminate a common theme.

The poems, taken simply on the surface, are about Milton himself, his tastes, his hobbies, his interests, viewed in terms of a relaxed young scholar, living in a beautiful countryside without any pressing tensions or involvements. It is a world seen and particularly *heard* from a fixed habitat, the scholar's study. The poet, exemplifying a long English tradition, is a walker. Sometimes the upland hamlets will "invite," and at another time he beholds the wandering moon on "the dry, smooth-shaven Green." The poet is not involved as an active participant in his environment, either as a sportsman or as a farmer. No other per-

Ideas in the Poems

son appears, though we hear hounds and horn and see groups of countrymen dancing in "the checkered shade." The point of view is that of a detached observer, a gentleman, a sensitive poet, a scholar on sabbatical.

Milton is sensitive to the slightest movements in the natural world, though he is not in these poems directly related to people:

> To hear the Lark begin his flight,
> And singing startle the dull night,
> From his watch-tow'r in the skies,
> Till the dappled dawn doth rise. . . .
> ("L'Allegro" 41–44)

The early-rising poet captures the spirit of a scene with brilliant verbal exactitude and with the ear of a musician. "Startle" is the action word that contrasts with the slow awakening of the total scene, and the adjective "dappled" has never been used so well before or since—the exactly right brush stroke, utterly economic. During the day, besides surveying actual living country pastoral (Corydon, Thyrsis, Thestylis), he reads Shakespeare, Ben Jonson, and Edmund Spenser ("linked sweetness long drawn out").

The night scenes of "Il Penseroso" have less in the way of extrinsic elaboration (such as the pastoral and Faery Mab accounts in "L'Allegro") and much more of what deeply and personally touched him. Vocation in "Il Penseroso" replaces holiday in "L'Allegro." Milton feels immediately attuned to the Cherub Contemplation and to Philomel, "Sweet Bird that shunn'st the noise of folly" (61). He watches the embers in the fire at dusk, hearing water from a distance, "swinging slow with sullen roar." He will read the night through in "some high lonely Tow'r," apparently without the need of human companionship. He will read Plato, Hermes Trismegistus, Greek tragedy, medieval chivalry and romance. He will welcome a dawn of wind and rain and will seek solitude in a virgin forest of "Pine or monumental Oak." He will walk in the studious cloister, listen to the pealing organ, dissolve into "ecstasies." From his immersion in profound religious experience, he hopes to reach "something like Prophetic strain."

But underlying the rather charming autobiographical revelations of the poems is a theme that was important to Milton and to the Renaissance—the meaning of *true* joy and *true* melancholy. "L'Allegro" and "Il Penseroso" actually present two kinds of joy and two kinds of melancholy. In each category, one kind is good and healthful; the other dangerous and evil. There is "loathed Melancholy / Of Cerberus and blackest midnight born" ("L'Allegro" 1–2) and "divinest Melancholy," "pensive Nun, devout and pure." The theme of the companion pieces is not merely a contrast between joy and melancholy, but a *quadruple* distinction between two kinds of joy and two kinds of melancholy.

The psychological distinctions involved in these companion pieces offer a parallel to those made in Robert Burton's *Anatomy of Melancholy*, a widely read book that had gone through many editions. Burton presents a "good" melancholy and a "bad" melancholy, in many respects similar to the difference Burton also makes between true religion and superstition. There is also a wise mirth (Milton's "joy"), which is recreative and healthful, and a false mirth, which leads to immorality and a neglect of duty.

The theme of "L'Allegro" is the replacement of "loathed Melancholy" by "heart-easing Mirth." In one section of Burton's *Anatomy*, entitled *Mind Rectified*, it is stated that one way to cure the evil type of melancholy is by *catharsis*, "to drive out one passion with another, or by some contrary passion."[1] This

Ideas in the Poems

reminds one of the statement in the preface of *Samson Agonistes:* "for so in Physic things of melancholic hue and quality are us'd against melancholy. . . ." But Burton's preferred method is: "Avoid over-much study and perturbations of the mind, and, as much as in thee lies, live at heart's ease."[2] "Mirth . . . purgeth the blood, confirms health, causes a fresh, pleasing and fine color, prorogues life, whets wit, makes the body young, lively and fit for any manner of employment."[3] Burton's doctrine is presented in a mosaic of quotations, and many contrasting views are apparent through these quotations. A discriminating reader (Milton, let us say) could make a consistent pattern of method and principle from such quotations as would win his approval.

It is to be noted that Milton in "L'Allegro" thinks of country sports, music, reading of comedy as defenses against the evil melancholy, just as Burton does. Burton mentions tilts and tournaments as being suitable "disports," and shortly thereafter makes an identical list of those enjoyments which Milton mentions in the lines beginning "Tow'red Cities please us then" ("L'Allegro" 117 ff.). Milton speaks of the medieval tournaments, "With store of Ladies, whose bright eyes / Rain influence, and judge the prize. . . ." One is reminded of Burton's quotations about woman: "Beauty alone is a sovereign remedy against wear, grief, and all melancholy fits."[4] He claims that "the sight of excellent beauties, attires, ornaments, delightsome passages" distracts melancholy minds from fear and sorrow. Burton includes in his list of winter recreations "tales of errant knights, queens, lovers, lords, ladies . . . dwarfs, witches, fairies, goblins. . . ."[5] Such stories are referred to in "L'Allegro." Milton makes a catalogued distinction between the pleasures of a day in the country and those of the night. Burton makes practically the same distinctions. One section of Burton's book contains a number of observations on music as a remedy against melancholy. He mentions the "sweet voices of children, Ionic and Lydian tunes exquisite music."⁶ This is analogous to Milton's "Lap me in soft Lydian Airs." As far as one can see, the only elements in "L'Allegro" which do not have correspondence in Burton are the references to the mountain nymph, "Sweet Liberty" (a distinctly Miltonic idea), and the references to Shakespeare and Ben Jonson.

But the important clues to Milton's theme are to be found in those passages where Burton deals with melancholy. The opening of "L'Allegro"—"Hence, loathed Melancholy"—suggests a number of analogies in Burton, and in particular Burton's theories of melancholy. Burton presents material that must have appealed to Milton enormously. The title of one section in Burton is "*Religious Melancholy. Its object God; what his beauty is; how it allureth. The parts and parties affected.*"⁷ In this section, the two kinds of melancholy are presented. The good melancholy, which is to be associated with the contemplation of beauty, leads to the contemplation of God; "other beauties are night itself, mere darkness, to this our inexplicable, incomprehensible, unspeakable, eternal, infinite, admirable and divine beauty." Burton speaks of "these spiritual eyes of contemplation," and shows how the love of God is secured through meditation and contemplation (see Chapter VI on the baroque).

The good melancholy, which Milton hails in "Il Penseroso" as "divinest Melancholy," leads to the *ecstasis* or ecstasy so beloved by the baroque thinkers of the seventeenth century and is defined as *divine* melancholy by Burton himself: "Ecstasis is a taste of future happiness, by which we are united unto God, a divine melancholy, a spiritual wing."⁸ In the same passage Burton distinguishes this "divine" melancholy from the evil melancholy: "But as it is abused, a mere dotage, a madness, a cause and symptom of Religious Melancholy." Looking at the opening

Ideas in the Poems

lines of "L'Allegro," one finds other parallels to Burton. The phrase "in dark Cimmerian desert ever dwell" is paralleled by Burton's reference to the "power of superstition in keeping people blind in *Cimmerian darkness.*" We have in the beginning of "L'Allegro" references to horrid shapes, to shrieks, to Stygian cave (hell), uncouth cell. All these phrases echo Burton, where he deals with despair arising out of religious melancholy:

> . . . a most intolerable pain and grief of heart seizeth on them: to their thinking they are already damned, they suffer the pains of Hell, and more than can possibly be expressed, they smell brimstone, talk familiarly with Devils, hear and see Chimeras, prodigious, uncouth shapes, Bears, Owls, Anticks, black dogs, fiends, hideous out-cries, fearful noises, shrieks, lamentable complaints, they are possessed, and through impatience they roar and howl, curse, blaspheme, deny God, call his power in question, abjure Religion, and are still ready to offer violence to themselves.[9]

Milton draws both verbal suggestions and ideas from Burton's *Anatomy*. Thus the "loathed Melancholy" of "L'Allegro," as the melancholy arising out of religious superstition, and the "divinest Melancholy," which leads to the perception of the beauty of God, are both fully explained in Burton. "Heart-easing Mirth" is the lawful distraction and pleasure which the pensive man can undertake to keep himself balanced and "lively and fit for any manner of employment." The "vain, deluding joys" mentioned in the beginning of "Il Penseroso" are the pleasures undertaken to relieve melancholy but which may dangerously become ends in themselves.

The companion pieces of "L'Allegro" and "Il Penseroso," then, can be better understood in the light of Burton's distinctions. Milton definitely makes a choice—that of the humanist who chooses the solitude and contemplation of the noble soul, the divine melancholy. Solitude was regarded in Milton's time with spiritual respect.[10] The seventeenth century did not connect the idea of solitude with loneliness ("for solitude is sometimes best society," *Paradise Lost* IX, 249). On the other hand, Milton is a humanist rather than a hermit, one who is balanced enough to enjoy the innocent pleasures and the beauty of the rural world. He has made a choice of vocation where all the synthesized aspects of life serve a final purpose:

> Till old experience do attain
> To something like Prophetic strain.
> ("Il Penseroso" 173–174)

THE IDEAS OF MODERATION AND EXCESS IN COMUS

Just as the soul can respond either to a divine or to an ignoble melancholy, as analyzed in regard to "L'Allegro" and "Il Penseroso," so we can respond to nature—the elusive and seductive sexuality of which is so well indicated in the lush summer night of *Comus*—either in a way that its power and beauty can be synthesized in the higher life of moderation and right reason, or so that we become part of a bacchantic madness.

In the union of lushness and restraint which Milton lyrically presents in the nature setting in *Comus*, we see a strong sense of humanistic order imposed on the fertile and the fecund. Milton has an extreme sensitivity to color, dimension, sound, but he particularly intuited a kind of sad nostalgia in nature. Nature is pointing to something else, beyond itself; nature is not complete, it is transitory, it is itself a pilgrim, a sad votarist:

> They left me then, when the gray-hooded Ev'n
> Like a sad votarist in Palmer's weed
> Rose from the hindmost wheels of Phoebus' wain.
> (188–190)

Ideas in the Poems

For Milton, even amid the tumult of beauty in Paradise, moments of reverence were present especially in the *muted* operations of nature:

> Now came still Ev'ning on, and Twilight gray
> Had in her sober Livery all things clad. . . .
> (*Paradise Lost* IV, 599–600)

In *Comus* nature is pregnant with mysterious spiritual movements—those of the lush and dank evening yet with a suggested cool of northern latitudes. Reassuring twilight is mingled with menacing, mysterious blackness. In a simple movement of the landscape, Milton can concentrate suspense and fear:

> Was I deceiv'd, or did a sable cloud
> Turn forth her silver lining on the night?
> I did not err, there does a sable cloud
> Turn forth her silver lining on the night,
> And casts a gleam over this tufted Grove.
> (221–225)

It is amazing the way in which Milton's imagery in this poem concentrates the psychological movement of drama in terse symbols of music and of the movement of sound. Thus Comus refers to the notes of the Echo song:

> How sweetly did they float upon the wings
> Of silence, through the empty-vaulted night,
> At every fall smoothing the Raven down
> Of darkness till it smil'd. . . .
> (250–253)

The almost liturgical movement of sounds in nature sustains the tension of the drama even more than do the characters themselves. The characters are like a chorus putting into words a drama that is occurring elsewhere. Nothing that the characters do is so intensely rich and tense as the following description of a symbolic sound:

> At last a soft and solemn-breathing sound
> Rose like a stream of rich distill'd Perfumes,
> And stole upon the Air, that even Silence
> Was took ere she was ware, and wish't she might
> Deny her nature, and be never more
> Still to be so displac't. I was all ear,
> And took in strains that might create a soul
> Under the ribs of Death. . . .
>
> (555–562)

Here is a powerful sexual and fertility reference, symbolized in music which is so sudden and complete in its germinative power that it creates a soul "under the ribs of death." This is a poetic statement that surpasses the dimensions of any stage action.

In this world of lushness and yet of control, the atmosphere is pervaded with tension. The theme is chastity—not a negative, mechanical chastity, but a vibrant, creative one. It is a "solemn vision" symbolized in sound that no gross ear can hear but of the most exquisite and all-enveloping tone for those who are rightly attuned. This is the world of "the unpolluted temple of the mind," of the "soul's essence." The apex of such a synthesis of light and sound is so reached that it is casually irrelevant whether the sun and moon "were in the flat sea sunk." This is a secret world, even beyond nature herself, the world toward which nature is a "votarist" and a "palmer," the world of grace. It is a world of grace where chastity has "sun-clad power," but of a sun beyond the sun.

In ironic contrast, Comus tries to dominate by power, by enchantment, what he only partially understands. Though he argues with the Lady with some dignity, basically he has something of the blurred vision of life that a small boy might learn in dark alleyways. He has rejected both the Socratic world of education, where knowledge must lead to good, and the Christian world of grace. Yet it must be said for him that he is compelled to admire what he cannot understand. He has to recognize, as Milton's Satan has to do, how awful goodness is and in her shape how lovely. Unlike Satan he has a zest for life, but, unable to draw on the sources of light, he is presented against a background of willful immaturity, of eccentric music in terms of artistically effective licentious imagery, of emotional abandonment, "blabbing scouts," "cabin'd loopholes," and the "telltale sun"—an atmosphere of perversion, secrecy, and an ironically roisterous sterility.

Comus, besides being superficially a masque, is even more a medieval debate. But it is a debate paradoxically maintained not so much by argumentation but by contrasting and most delicately attuned poetic images. A remarkable synthesis is achieved, reminiscent of what Edmund Spenser had in mind but failed to effect. Spenser was extremely sensitive to the pagan combination of beauty and grace with sensuality. It might be said that, to some extent, he compromised both the reader and himself. Who does not feel at times that the destruction of the Bower of Bliss by Sir Guyon and the Palmer is somewhat brutal and "wanton" (in another sense of this ambiguous word)? If an artist succeeds in making sin too attractive, he then cannot escape the impression of being insincere when he sets out to condemn it. To know and yet to abstain requires a very fine intellectual balance. Milton has succeeded in giving warmth as well as meaning to an artistically perilous theme.

The sage and serious doctrine of virginity is correlated to, though not concomitant with or essentially dependent upon, the Renaissance role of noble solitude, the active and creative contemplation of the melancholy man in the great and good sense delineated in "Il Penseroso." Some light can be thrown on Milton's view of virginity by his Platonic background. Socrates had viewed human relations eschatologically in the *Symposium*. Man, his thesis is, desires everlasting possession of the good, and all men will desire immortality with the good. Universal love in regard to offspring is for the sake of immortality. But wisdom and virtue, justice and temperance are more honorable offspring than mortal children. While Socrates does not impose virginity as a condition for the ascent of the ladder of perfection, one moves from various experiences to an ultimate point of view that is virginal in respect to the relationship of the soul to God. An eloquent passage (disturbing only to those Christians who find incarnational truths bypassed) should be quoted, for it is likely that it influenced Milton more than (certainly as much as) any medieval traditions about the meaning of virginity. The soul, in the Socratic view, ultimately seeks a beauty, absolute, separate, simple, and everlasting, which—without diminution or increase, or any change—is imparted to the ever-growing and perishing beauty of other things.

> "He who from these ascending under the influence of true love begins to perceive that beauty is not far from the end. And the true order of going, or being led by another, to the things of love, is to begin from the beauties of earth and mount upwards for the sake of that other beauty, using these as steps only, and from one going on to two, and from two to all fair forms, and from fair forms to fair practices, and from fair practices to fair notions, until from fair notions he arrives at the notion of absolute beauty, and at last knows what the essence of beauty is. This, my dear Socrates," said the stranger of Mantinea, "is that life above all others which man should live, in the contemplation of beauty absolute.... Remember how in that communion only, beholding beauty with the eye of the mind, he will be

enabled to bring forth, not images of beauty, but realities (for he has hold not of an image but of a reality), and bringing forth and nourishing true virtue to become the friend of God and be immortal, if mortal man may."[11]

The Elder Brother in speaking of "Saintly chastity" echoes this thinking:

> So dear to Heav'n is Saintly chastity
> That when a soul is found sincerely so,
> A thousand liveried Angels lackey her,
> Driving far off each thing of sin and guilt,
> And in clear dream and solemn vision
> Tell her of things that no gross ear can hear,
> Till oft converse with heav'nly habitants
> Begin to cast a beam on th'outward shape,
> The unpolluted temple of the mind,
> And turns it by degrees to the soul's essence,
> Till all be made immortal. . . .
> (453–463)

Some critics have maintained that an underlying theme of the *Comus* is the relationship of nature to grace. Is the Lady sufficiently tempted to have to go beyond the resources of nature, of the natural virtue of temperance, to draw upon a heaven-gifted strength? Arthur S. P. Woodhouse argues that Milton would not have been sympathetic to extremes either of asceticism or of naturalism.[12] Woodhouse accepts the medieval tradition, an important revision of Aristotelianism, that temperance is a virtue of the natural order and chastity is a virtue of the supernatural order. He also contends that chastity forms a link between temperance in the natural order and virginity, which belongs to the supernatural order. Comus, according to Woodhouse, is a bad logician in the natural order because he attacks temperance.

Ideas in Milton

The idea of virginity obviously included that of chastity, but the idea of chastity included both that of virginity and of marriage. Spenser had symbolized chastity in the person of Britomart who ultimately was to marry Artegall. He had attempted to synthesize the Christian traditions of both marriage and virginity in his symbolic narrative of the Garden of Adonis (*The Faerie Queene* III, vi) by placing them on an equal level. The Christian theory of virginity was a complex one and raises difficult problems in several fields of theology. Virginity had been thought of as eschatological in purpose, symbolizing that Christ's kingdom was not of this world. It was frequently assumed in literature on the subject that the instinct, naturally good, of the virgin is toward marriage, that marriage is a noble good and it is only at the insistence of a higher good through a specific vocation of divine grace that this good must yield to something still higher. The higher good of consecrated virginity was, in turn, often symbolized as a spiritual marriage.

That pagans could maintain a life of virginity and chastity is illustrated by the vestal virgins and other religious groups of ancient times. One critic has observed of the Lady in *Comus* that to "make her virtue wholly dependent on heaven's assistance would scarcely be an overwhelming compliment to pay her," adding that "one simply does not tell an earl's daughter that she is chaste only by the grace of God."[13] The Christian, of course, does not live by nature alone and then call upon grace only when necessity arises. He lives both a life of nature and of grace, the latter being, according to medieval thought, the fulfillment, not the contradiction, of nature. It does not follow that natural virtue would be inadequate without special grace—this would presumably depend upon the stress and strain of circumstance: "Or if Virtue feeble were / Heav'n itself would stoop to her" (1022–1023).

Ideas in the Poems

Milton has an unresolved problem in *Comus*, because the theme of virginity reflects the noble solitude of the contemplative as in "Il Penseroso," but there is no reason to suppose that the Lady has so specific a virginal vocation (in so far as she is to be identified with the Earl of Bridgewater's daughter, socially destined for marriage, certainly not—and we must remember that the *Comus* was written for a special occasion). Critics have pointed out that certain lines, not in the Trinity manuscript of 1634 but added in the printed version of 1637, indicate a modification of a narrow doctrine of virginity. Milton in these lines recalls Spenser's Garden of Adonis (*The Faerie Queene* III, vi). Chrysogone had conceived and given birth to twin daughters, Belphoebe and Amoret, in a sleep without pain. A nymph of Diana (goddess of chastity) found them and bore them away while their mother was still sleeping. Diana adopted Belphoebe and brought her up to be a beautiful virgin warrior. Amoret, on the other hand, destined for marriage, was brought up by Venus in the sanctuary of the Garden of Adonis. Amoret married Sir Scudamour and was to have children. Preceding the lines is a deliberate exhortation—"List, mortals, if your ears be true"—which may indicate that Milton wanted to stress his meaning:

> (List mortals, if your ears be true)
> Beds of Hyacinth and Roses
> Where young Adonis oft reposes,
> Waxing well of his deep wound
> In slumber soft, and on the ground
> Sadly sits th' Assyrian Queene;
> But far above in spangled sheen
> Celestial Cupid her fam'd son advanc't,
> Holds his dear Psyche sweet intranc't
> After her wand'ring labors long,
> Till free consent the gods among

> Make her his eternal Bride,
> And from her fair unspotted side
> Two blissful twins are to be born,
> Youth and joy; so Jove hath sworn.
> (997–1011)

The Garden of Adonis constitutes an erotic reference, and Milton seems to have felt it necessary to modify his doctrine of virginity to include marriage. In her relationship to Comus, the Lady triumphed as Belphoebe; but, having triumphed as Belphoebe, she is free to proceed to her true part of Amoret.[14]

The success of Comus does not lie in its extended debate between excess and moderation, in its definition of ideas. It lies in its pattern of imagery which effectively dramatizes the human situation torn by the seductiveness of natural beauty and its responsibility to go beyond what is transitory and find "that Golden Key / That opes the Palace of Eternity" (13–14). The nature that Milton has described in the poem has greater powers for good or evil, dependent on whether we meet them with excess or temperance, than anything Comus has to offer. Comus himself is not seductive, though he has a lyrical appreciation of natural beauty. Milton succeeds as an artist in conveying the more subtle and sensitive aspects of nature so that we are sympathetically drawn to their triumph, as symbols of moderation and temperance, over any excess that Comus can justify by argument. But there is sufficient of Comus in Milton himself so that the victory of virtue is not annihilating; we understand poetically what is wrong in the Comus attitude while remaining appreciative of the beauty and fertility of nature. In effect, the sage and serious doctrine of virginity underlies any understanding of the total relationship of things, including the bounty of nature and marriage itself. Such relationships cannot be forced by magic or by power; they must be spontaneous and free, retaining their own identity.

THE RELIGIOUS VISION OF "LYCIDAS"

In the "Lycidas," Milton still expresses some apprehension as to whether he is quite ready to take up the high vocation of poet for which he has prepared himself for so long. But he cannot avoid the compelling occasion of the death of a fellow student, Edward King. We are told with echoing pathos that Lycidas is dead, the *young* Lycidas, who has not left his peer. He himself was a poet, and it is partly on this basis that Milton finds so close an affinity with him. They have shared a camaraderie of education, ancient culture, and a practice of the great art of poetry:

> For we were nurst upon the self-same hill,
> Fed the same flock, by fountain, shade, and rill.
> (23–24)

The reader associates with these lines the timeless classical image of leisurely days devoted to high pursuits, far from the hard labors and petty frustrations that so often afflict the sons of men. We are reminded by a reference to his beloved tutor ("And old Damaetas lov'd to hear our song," 36) of the English university's tutorial system with its intimate contact between a teacher and his small number of scholars.

Another note is rung on the change to a different type of pathos—a sense of affection, a sense of nostalgia, of loneliness, and of something past and done:

> But O the heavy change, now thou art gone,
> Now thou art gone, and never must return!
> (37–38)

Ideas in Milton

His poetry is no longer there for nature to respond to, and the charm of generations of pastorals is alluded to in the familiar images of the civilized English countryside. The references to the wild thyme, the gadding vine, the willow, the hazel copses, the whitethorn recall all the familiar objects of an intimate and domestic natural scene.

Milton, except in those instances (chiefly in *Paradise Regained* and *Samson Agonistes*) where a certain Puritanism gains the upper hand, is a synthesizer in the great tradition of men of the Renaissance, as, for example, Edmund Spenser. They combine the natural scene, the routine of rustic living, with the overtones, especially the musical harmonies, of the ancient classics. Milton is preoccupied with the poet as the guide and conductor of civilization. He makes a central use of the image of Orpheus as a bridge to the discussion of the "homely slighted Shepherd's trade" (65) of poetry. Orpheus, when he has been rejected and physically dismembered by one society and his members cast upon the waters, is retrieved and given honored burial in another world which is to renew the ever-pressing conflict against decadence. But always the high stream of poetic thought continues to flow somewhere in our world:

> What could the Muse herself that Orpheus bore,
> The Muse herself, for her enchanting son
> Whom Universal nature did lament,
> When by the rout that made the hideous roar,
> His gory visage down the stream was sent,
> Down the swift Hebrus to the Lesbian shore?
> (58–63)

The harshness of angry decadence is well suggested in the harsh alliteration of the line: "When by the *rout* that made the hideous *roar*." And an indication of the enormity of the crime and the grandeur of the redemption is conveyed in the type of line at

Ideas in the Poems

which Milton is so adept—that of vast geographical suggestiveness: "Down the swift Hebrus to the Lesbian shore."

The poem contains, as some of the later Renaissance pastorals do, a good deal of personal social criticism. Milton thinks of the thankless pursuit of the noble art of poetry. Would it not be better to live a life of elegant amusement than tend the homely, slighted shepherd's trade? The answer may lie in the mirage of reputation. Here Milton expresses one of the great insistent themes of the Renaissance—the pursuit of fame, the fame that so inspired the Greek world, the desire to gain immortality on the lips of men by high achievement. But Milton is a serious Christian, and the value of a Christian person does not lie on the lips of men but in his relationship to God.

"Fame is the spur that the clear spirit doth raise" (70), and, in this sense, it is a noble thing. Yet, set against the grandeur of the Christian dispensation, it is a kind of weakness, "that last infirmity of Noble mind" (71). The pathos of classical ambitions is always related to the inevitable fact of death, for, even when temporal fame is gained, it is likely to give only an ephemeral satisfaction to the man who has won it. But Christianity has offered mankind a higher hope, that of immortality, and this is the fame, judged in terms of so tremendous a value, that a Christian must pursue. It must be the fame that springs from "the witness of all-judging Jove" (82). Milton, though deeply imbued with classical humanism, does not forget its limitations within the terms of the Christian vision.

Milton, who himself had thought of the possibility of a clerical vocation, then presents a severe criticism of the clergy. In a few powerful words he expresses feelings of tense indignation about the corruption of religion from the point of view of one who takes religion with profound seriousness. He is castigating those who pursue a clerical career simply out of selfish egoism, without real concern for people who are hungry for serious spiritual guidance. What could sum up Milton's object of contempt better than the brilliant mixed metaphor, *"blind mouths"* (119) —pastors who are intellectually blind but whose greed is almost a physical quality?[15] It is the reverse side of that deeply felt religious conviction that gives emotional unity to the entire work.

Milton assures us of the artistic intention of the piece. He realizes there are a variety of moods in this piece and indicates that he is prepared to combine them, for he says, "the dread voice is past / That shrunk thy streams" (132–133). He breaks into a different strain as he creates the touching beauty of the flower passage, with its mixture of native English wildflowers (crow-toe, pansy, glowing violet) and the amaranthus, the classical flower of immortality that grows on the other side of the grave.

Then comes the thought: Where indeed are the mortal remains of Lycidas? Milton gives a powerful vision of the physical immensity of nature, the might of the sea which can be violent and chaotic, tearing apart all humanism, classical and Christian:

> Whether beyond the stormy Hebrides,
> Where thou perhaps under the whelming tide
> Visit'st the bottom of the monstrous world. . . .
> (156–158)

The vast image of negative power causes the poet to look to the supernatural for pity; this is a sorrow that merits the compassion of angels:

> Look homeward Angel now, and melt with ruth:
> And, O ye Dolphins, waft the hapless youth.
> (163–164)

We have a variety of moods—pathos, indignation, reassurance. These are human emotions, but the deep Christian vision of

Ideas in the Poems

Milton in this poem is not satisfied with them. Ultimately, human contradictions, human frustrations, the human sense that somehow essential questions have been missed or left unanswered have to be met by that form of knowledge which goes by the name of Faith—the "unexpressive [inexpressible] nuptial song" of Christ. That is the world of ultimate reconciliation, and King himself becomes an agent of the redemptive power of Providence set against a world of aggression, selfishness, and death:

> Henceforth thou art the Genius of the shore,
> In thy large recompense, and shalt be good
> To all that wander in that perilous flood.
> (183–185)

For those who remain here, who still have their race to run, the poetic image implies that somehow the shocking and tragic aspects of talent unfulfilled, vocations that go nowhere, are only of temporary importance. Life continues, and Providence still works its way in the everyday world. The narrating shepherd goes on his path, at peace and relieved:

> Thus sang the uncouth Swain to th'Oaks and rills,
> While the still morn went out with Sandals gray. . . .
> (186–187)

"Still morn with Sandals gray" is an image of universal nature at peace and rest, working its own benediction, an image of that divine peace of the "blest Kingdoms meek of joy and love" (177). Milton suggests the quiet joy in the narrator:

> He touch't the tender stops of various Quills,
> With eager thought warbling his Doric lay. . . .
> (188–189)

"Lycidas" is remarkable for the change and variety of its moods, which are united by an inner psychology and an inner aptness, largely determined by the ancient wisdom of Christian tradition. The poem is characterized by an unusual sense of harmony and reconciliation, subtle in its orchestration and in the illusive force of its poetry. A spirit of reverence and a resolution of internal tensions are manifested beyond the usual routines of experience, thought, study. Something indeed has fallen upon the poem like a benediction, something like the music of the spheres to which Milton so often alludes. It is an omnipresent atmosphere but difficult to define in so many words.

One obvious quality is the great classical sense of repose. We find this in Greek sculpture where the form itself indicates an enormous depth of feeling, but where there is not one touch too much of emotional exaggeration, one detail that is superfluous. In this poem there is some solemnity of the human spirit, something living and breathing, no longer the victim of flux and change. "Lycidas" is full of illusive messages that float like clouds, partly concealing and partly revealing a lofty mountain peak, accentuating by contrast its sharp and rugged strength. For "Lycidas" is not a pastoral in the sense of rural escape, a kind of lofty moment of serene recreation. It has struck deeply into the world of tragedy in its sense of harmony and reconcilement.

If it transcends the pagan desire of fame, it also transcends the Christian's capacity for social indignation. It is a poem fully alive, full of tension, and yet it is able to attain a serenity of religious peace. All the traditions of the past speak here in a new synthesis; all the associations going back to classical and medieval times, all the new grandeurs of the Renaissance, combine here in a poignant and controlled way.

It might well be argued that "Lycidas" conveys the impression of the most deeply *felt* religious thought of all of Milton's poetry, even deeper and richer in its inner feeling, at least more concentrated, than *Paradise Lost*. Milton presents a religious

Ideas in the Poems

view in terms of beauty, sincerity, and hallowed tradition, both classical and Christian. It is assertive and affirmative in the manner of noble poetic statement, unmarred by discursive theological argumentation. The frame of reference is also truly human, as seen in the imaging forth of a reconciling and healing divine Providence, unimpeded by any suggestion of the cruxes of theological polemics. The poem belongs to the world of ritual, of public beauty, and does not retire, as *Paradise Lost* sometimes does, to the theological seminar.

The beauty of the poem actually consoles, in a spiritual as well as an aesthetic sense. One is led to feel the presence of a power, however mysterious and undefined, that is truly right, and *right* throughout the universe—and, moreover, communicable to human beings in terms to which they can respond through love to a divine love that is uncensorious, that delights in its own being and in our being. Milton's religious sense in this work far surpasses any intellectual mode; it is instinctive, intuitive, expressing a redemptive image that radiates through and transforms intellection and verbalization, even in the face of outright negation, as in the case of the corrupted clergy. The inner strength of the piece is such as to assimilate and transcend the thoughts and feelings that might threaten its harmony. The harsh and indignant voice is essential to its beauty, just as Dante's Hell is essential to his assertion of Paradise, for such contrasts and oppositions serve to create dynamic rather than flat, unilateral statements. Today the recognized word for this kind of artistic process is *tension*. In the final analysis "Lycidas" is not a poem of several moods but of one mood, one overriding tension, transcending and reconciling opposites.

This work comes closest in Milton to that medieval personal devotional note which is sometimes lacking elsewhere. Christ is more vividly present here, where he does not enter as a character, than in *Paradise Lost* where he does. One critic has pointed out, "Each aspect of 'Lycidas' poses the question of premature death as it relates to the life of man, of poetry, and of the church. But all these aspects are contained within the figure of Christ, the young dying God who is eternally alive, the Word that contains all poetry, the head and body of the church, the good shepherd whose pastoral world sees no winter, the Sun of Righteousness that never sets, whose power can raise Lycidas, like Peter, out of the waves, as it redeems souls from the lower world, which Orpheus failed to do. Christ does not enter the poem as a character but he pervades every line of it."[16] Another commentator observes, "Upon the literal level of pagan pastoralism we superimpose, as it were, our fuller Christian understanding, and we see what the uncouth swain cannot see, that the fragmentary symbols of rebirth and immortality scattered through the pastoral landscape are gathered up into the perfect image of Christ. . . ."[17]

THE IMAGES OF CHRIST AND SATAN IN PARADISE REGAINED

A certain Miltonic note very much present in the companion pieces, in *Comus*, in "Lycidas," and still at the forefront of *Paradise Lost* is no longer heard in *Paradise Regained* and *Samson Agonistes*. Milton's ever available lyricism is gone, though there might be solid artistic reasons for not employing lyricism in the latter two works. But more important, there is some loss of magnanimity in regard to the human situation. Milton's central point of view has become more harsh, more sectarian, basically less classical (in spite of the external form of *Samson Agonistes*), and more Puritanical. His generalized statements are often more

Ideas in the Poems

flat and unilateral, less imagistic. Something seems to have weakened, perhaps died, in the great humanistic synthesis of Milton, and though he still has great riches to offer as commentators in the history of ideas tradition amply point out, there is a decline in poetic drive and fire.[18]

Milton is certainly less ambiguous in *Paradise Regained* and *Samson Agonistes* than in what are generally agreed to be his earlier major poems. But great art seems to be distinguished by a certain amount of ambiguity. Shakespeare wrote both *King Lear* and *Timon of Athens*; both deal with the theme of ingratitude. But we are never certain about our judgments of Lear; he gives rise to many questions. The statement about Timon is unilateral and dull. Major critics have devoted major studies to Lear; hardly anyone has wasted time on Timon. While this is not conclusive proof of anything, *Paradise Regained* has remained incapable of attracting anywhere near the critical attention accorded *Paradise Lost*, although both deal with the central theme of temptation. Temptation in *Paradise Lost* is related to the human condition, ambiguous, and artistically convincing. Temptation in the *Paradise Regained* seems remote, partaking more of a theological debate than a real human involvement.[19]

The central difficulty of *Paradise Regained* lies in the characterization of Christ, though the Satan of the piece is a different character, with different motivations, than the Satan of the major epic. The problem in *Paradise Regained* is that it would be theologically unpermissible for Christ to display at any time any interior flaw. It is very difficult to find the temptations convincing rather than merely ritualistic. *Paradise Lost* could not have been successful if Adam had not had the potentiality for sin. One critic finds in Milton the persistence of a Renaissance tradition that the temptation was one of the occasions on which Christ was "affected chiefly and most visibly in his human nature."[20]

It is true that in this poem Milton places almost exclusive emphasis on Christ as man, but as man without vulnerability and, therefore, undramatic. It has been argued, on a quasi-theological level, that Satan's primary objective was to seek reliable information: Was this man indeed the Messiah? This view, however, will still leave us with a similar artistic problem. If Satan had succeeded, then he would not have been dealing with the Christ, and, consequently, the narrative about regaining Paradise would fall apart. If Satan does not succeed, he is then dealing with a Christ who is effectively above temptation and undramatic as we mentioned. If the narrative shows simply a research exploration on the part of Satan, the theme is even more obviously shadowboxing, though at least Satan, in trying to tempt an untemptable Christ, is an ironic character.

In many ways, Milton's hands are more tied here by his basic material than they were in *Paradise Lost* by Genesis, for Genesis is a mythic statement or at least a poetic one, whereas the New Testament narrative was normally accepted as historical fact. Inventiveness on the part of the poet is less open to resentment in a poetic statement than in a historical account. It is one thing to give God the Father or Christ lengthy imagined speeches before human history is written; it imposes quite a different problem in credibility to put speeches of Milton's own creation into Christ's mouth after Christ has himself become immanent in history. It is extremely difficult to synthesize Christ in history with Christ as a partially fictional development without any violence or offence to historical material.

But this difficulty, great as it is, is less of an artistic problem than that arising from the presuppositions which would exist in the minds of readers from having been already acquainted with the *Paradise Lost*.

We had left Satan, for example, in Book X of *Paradise Lost* as a serpent among the other hissing serpents. But apparently this was no final denouement. Now we learn that Satan has appeared among the sons of God to make a sporting bet:

> I came among the Sons of God when he
> Gave up into my hands Uzzean Job
> To prove him. . . .
> *(Paradise Regained* I, 368–370)

He retains his capacity, in spite of his former epic degeneration, to admire what is beautiful and virtuous:

> . . . Though I have lost
> Much lustre of my native brightness, lost
> To be belov'd of God, I have not lost
> To love, at least contemplate and admire
> What I see excellent in good, or fair,
> Or virtuous. . . .
> (I, 377–382)

Christ argues that Satan is composed of lies, and that, in spite of everything he attempts, Satan is still serviceable to heaven's King (I, 421). Satan in *Paradise Regained* is a consistent, though simplified, character. He retains one feature of the epic Satan: his capacity for deception, and what he says cannot be accepted at face value. He has little of the adventurousness, little of the sense of inward struggle, little of the confused emotional response that make the epic devil of constant dramatic interest. The Satan of *Paradise Regained* has one, instead of several, dimensions.

In the portrayal of Christ we also have a set of associations quite different from those to which we are accustomed in *Paradise Lost*. In the epic, Christ is a military leader, the right-hand executive of the Father. Nothing in *Paradise Regained* would harmonize with the scene in Book VI of *Paradise Lost* of Christ driving his chariot through the midst of his enemies, at his right hand victory sitting eagle-winged. In *Paradise Regained* Christ actually objects to the "cumbersome luggage of war":

> ... argument
> Of human weakness rather than of strength.
> (III, 401–402)

Christ is here, in the words of Satan, "addicted more / to contemplation and profound dispute . . ." (IV, 213–214). In the midst of the most furious storms, spewing among other things "Infernal Ghosts and Hellish Furies," Christ "Satt'st unappall'd in calm and sinless peace" (IV, 425).

On the other hand, though Milton has dropped the military imagery associated with Christ in *Paradise Lost,* he has not been able to relate sufficiently the Christ of *Paradise Regained* to the Christ who volunteered to die for man (*Paradise Lost* III, 235–236). Perhaps because of Milton's increasing Arian tendencies, he presents a Christ who, plainly speaking, seems to have had amnesia in regard to his previous status described in the epic. Christ in the epic had foreknowledge; even Michael did. Here Christ has to learn everything from the beginning:

> And now by some strange motion I am led
> Into this Wilderness, to what intent
> I learn not yet; perhaps I need not know;
> For what concerns my knowledge God reveals.
> (I, 290–293)

The question arises whether the reader has a right to expect a continuity in characterization between the two Christs (and the two Satans) of *Paradise Lost* and *Paradise Regained.* Any such expectations are disappointed.

Both the material and the format of *Paradise Regained* are

artistically inhibiting. In comparison to the major epic, *Paradise Regained* lacks action and tension. Only two characters, Christ and Satan, are involved, compared with the much more crowded canvas of the epic, and neither character undergoes a major psychological or ideological change. In *Paradise Lost* we have the sense that Satan, Adam, Eve all change, grow, or degenerate in respect to a dynamic situation in which they have an active part.

Though the main episodes and their outcomes were known beforehand to the audience of *Paradise Lost*, Milton, like the Greek masters in their handling of legendary material, made the episodes suspenseful and created the illusion of beholding them for the first time. In *Paradise Regained*, as in the epic, we know that Milton may embellish but not deny the main lines of his story as told in his source material. But the material here has imposed certain conditions which Milton cannot find a means of avoiding. Since only two characters comprise the action, and since all that is done actually symbolizes various aspects of conflicting viewpoints and values, the reader cannot escape the impression that he is listening to a medieval debate rather than to a drama or narrative poem. *Comus* is also a debate but, in addition, a lively drama. Elaboration is no substitute for tension. It is interesting to contrast, for example, the tense and poignant drama on Adam learning of Eve's sin

> Astonied stood and Blank, while horror chill
> Ran through his veins, and all his joints relax'd;
> From his slack hand the Garland wreath'd for Eve
> Down dropp'd, and all the faded roses shed. . . .
> (*Paradise Lost* IX, 890–893)

with the elaborate banquet described in detail to tempt the fasting Christ (*Paradise Regained* II). Milton comments:

> Alas how simple, to these Cates compar'd,
> Was the crude Apple that diverted Eve!
> (II, 348-349)

But the artistic drawback here is that, however embellished the regal banquet prepared by Satan, the crude apple of *Paradise Lost* was intensely more dramatic.

SAMSON AGONISTES AND PURITANISM

In *Samson Agonistes* Milton returns to a good deal of the intransigence of the Old Testament and rejects many of the modifying impacts of humanism.

Virtue here is not that goodness characterizing the blaze of being embracing the creator and the created throughout the universe; virtue is the result of an intensely personal struggle in which an individual finally wins through to a personal triumph amid an environment that is openly inimical when it is not passive and sterile. It is a work that tells us more about the nobility of solitude than about the grandeur of man, more about Puritanism as the religion of the will than about that Hellenic cosmic harmony presided over by intelligence. If the play ends with "calm of mind, all passion spent," it is in terms of purgatorial suffering that is finished with. Goodness triumphs but in a lonely, separated, self-flagellating way. In respect to the *agon* of the drama, one critic has aptly defined its predominant characteristics: "Samson is in a sense another Adam, but an Adam more completely abandoned to the warfare of the elements, more bitterly frustrated, more mature in suffering. The resolution of the conflict, moreover, is on a different level from anything we have met elsewhere in Milton's work. Samson accomplishes his restoration to favor by his own effort. . . . Though the poem is religious, it is not right reason which triumphs but the will of man."[21]

Milton intends that the delineation of Samson's sufferings

Ideas in the Poems

shall end in a serene acceptance of the mysterious ways of God:

> Nothing is here for tears, nothing to wail
> Or knock the breast, no weakness, no contempt,
> Dispraise, or blame, nothing but well and fair
> And what may quiet us in a death so noble.
> (1721–1724)

But the question remains whether we gain a real interior vision from this somber drama: Are any dilemmas really resolved, or is light thrown on dilemmas still remaining unresolved? Or has something soured in the synthesis and cosmic vision that Milton achieved in *Paradise Lost*? What has happened to the humanistic interpretation of religious values, to the powerful synthesis of Christianity and classicism? To what extent is Milton in this document, which has a personally embittered side, exhibiting a retrogression to pure Puritanism? Is virtue, as presented in the play, something separating one man from another rather than uniting men? Is the play classical in form rather than in spirit?

First of all, we have to keep in mind that Milton's choice of Samson as a subject was not individualistic or eccentric. While any cursory reading of the Book of Judges would indicate to most people that Samson is a character of very doubtful attractiveness, a vast amount of scriptural exegesis had prepared the seventeenth century for a much more symbolic, much nobler Samson. Samson belongs to the Old Testament tradition of the Nazir, a man dedicated to God from his mother's womb. Such a man's birth had unusual, even miraculous, characteristics. Samson, like St. John the Baptist, was born to a woman past the normal child-bearing age. His birth was foretold by an angel. A Nazir was bound to be even stricter than the already strict laws observed by all Hebrews. He cannot touch a dead thing, nor take strong drink; he cannot cut his hair, symbol of strength.

The Savior, at least on the surface, was a Nazir as well as a rabbi. On this level, a very old analogy between Samson and Christ could be maintained. But there are episodes in the biblical account of Samson that are difficult to harmonize with any religious symbolism or even any sense of justice (for example, Samson's marrying a girl in order to destroy her family, or killing thirty men to pay off a bet).

The symbolical interpretation of biblical narratives had gone to extremes. Hugo of St. Victor had interpreted Samson's marriage to a Philistine as an image of Christ's foundation of his church among the Gentiles.[22] Augustine in his *Sermo de Samsone* finds that the companion to whom Samson's bride was given (Judges 15:20) signified the rise of heretics. The episode of Samson going into the harlot of Gaza (Judges 16:1) was a symbol of the harrowing of hell, of Christ in the bonds of death.[23]

Today we have an increased understanding of how the books of the Old Testament were put together. We have to imagine the Hebrew compiler as having a deep reverence for any tradition, oral or written. If several versions of the Samson story were available, including some folk tales like those of our own about Paul Bunyan, the Old Testament compiler simply put them all together. He was not like a contemporary professional editor or scholar who would attempt to collate his material, distinguishing what was authentic from what was not.

In the story of the Book of Judges, everything bearing on Samson is jammed together, whether religiously authentic or folklore. Milton underplays or merely refers in passing to the more unsavory aspects of the account of Samson. He uses almost half of the biblical account of Samson but has omitted details which he probably felt would not be suitable to a tragic hero.

Milton also makes important additions. He presents Dalila as Samson's wife. There is no indication of this in Scripture, but this change ennobles Samson and elevates Dalila to a more tragic personality. In the Book of Judges Dalila has someone else shave off Samson's hair, but in the drama she does it herself. Milton's drama differs from the Old Testament story in other respects; some of these differences were brought about by omissions and others by deliberate changes. There is no scriptural precedent for the visits of Manoa, Dalila, Harapha, and the officer.

It has been well argued by F. Michael Krouse in *Milton's Samson and the Christian Tradition* that Milton built on a historical basis which had already evolved a conception of Samson strikingly different from that afforded by the Book of Judges. Most of the material underlying this strictly different Samson is to be found in the hermeneutic, homiletic literature of early Christianity. "From the biblical commentaries, the sermons, the exempla and other writings of the fathers of the early church, the schoolmen of the late middle ages and the learned divines of the Renaissance we can describe and reconstruct the Samson tradition which lies behind and between the lines of Milton's tragedy, the attitude toward the hero which Milton expected his fit audience to have."[24]

The death of Samson was always a thorny problem. St. Augustine argues in the *De Civitate Dei* that saints are not necessarily to be imitated in all their acts and cites Samson, but he then goes on to justify Samson's self-destruction. He holds that Samson was an exceptional case because we know he was impelled by God.[25] Although it was generally conceded that Samson was a saint, the fact of his fall was universally acknowledged. It was generally argued that this fall was made allowable by God's concession and for God's own purposes. The history of the Christian exegesis of Samson helps to explain why, from the time when he first made plans to write a tragedy, Milton perceived a tragic hero in Samson, who seems on the surface to be only a tribal hero.

The analogy between Milton's own life and certain aspects of Samson's life is inescapable, if we assume a late date for the work. Milton had met a severe reversal of fortune. The Puritan revolution had run its course, and the Philistines (the Royalist Church-of-England group) were to be in control again. Milton, like Samson, is physically blind, and blind among *enemies*. But the parallel stops in the matter of guilt. Samson has betrayed his trust; Milton has not. Milton's sufferings are, in this respect, more like those of Job, less like those of Samson. But the emotions roused by both physical blindness and Philistian supremacy are just as much part of Milton's life as that of the stage character of Samson. So are the corresponding virtues of patience, endurance, determination, and courage. Both had been exiled from light—light, the prime work of God, extinct in both. In the absence of physical light, they had to deepen the resources of spiritual light.

Milton humanizes a good deal of the Samson material as he did with Genesis. He modifies the rather horrible purposefulness of Samson in the original where he marries a Philistian woman with the overt purpose of destroying her family. Samson, in Milton's version, does not proceed consciously on this level; he simply fulfills the will of God, the knowledge of which comes through direct illumination from the deity. In answer to the question why he married outside his tribe, the daughter of an infidel, Samson replies:

> . . . they knew not
> That what I motion'd was of God; I knew
> From intimate impulse, and therefore urg'd
> The Marriage on. . . .
>
> (221–224)

Ideas in the Poems

Milton also rationalizes Samson's slaying of thirty Philistines to satisfy the terms of a bet on the ground that they were military spies seeking through his bride to learn the conditions of his great strength (1196 ff.).

The relation of Samson to his God is very direct (like that of radical Protestantism), without the interposition of the senses, study, society. Samson's strength, though "heaven-gifted" (36), is unimportant in the sight of God, who directs Samson to an end of which he is not informed:

> God, when he gave me strength, to show withal
> How slight the gift was, hung it in my Hair.
> But peace, I must not quarrel with the will
> Of highest dispensation, which herein
> Haply had ends above my reach to know. . . .
> (58–62)

God does not work incarnationally through men or society; only direct relationship with him provides any comfort:

> Little prevails, or rather seems a tune,
> Harsh, and of dissonant mood from his complaint,
> Unless he feel within
> Some source of consolation from above. . . .
> (661–664)

Samson is a lonely man, who is separated from his wife, whose father and friends can do little or no good for him, and who has an oppressive sense of guilt about the misuse of his gift of strength. He images himself as the instrument of God, as "a person separate to God / Design'd for great exploits" (31–32). But wisdom was not granted to him as a gift of grace along with strength:

> But what is strength without a double share
> Of wisdom?
> (53–54)

It might be asked whether God himself was wise in giving Samson the one without the other (on a broader level we might ask a similar question about atomic power today), or did Milton mean that the acquiring of wisdom was man's own responsibility based on his own strivings? Arnold Stein in *Heroic Knowledge* seems to support the latter view in maintaining that "knowledge, the self-knowledge of thought tested by deed, heroic knowledge"[26] is the key theme of the drama. On the other hand, an inescapable theme in the play indicates that Samson's fall has not been due to lack of knowledge but to weakness in the face of female assault.

Critics have argued that Adam in *Paradise Lost* actually did the right thing in breaking God's commandment, for this act also generated the Redemption; similarly it could be argued that Samson's disobedience was ultimately responsible for the fall of the Philistines. In regard to Milton's thinking, this surmise is almost as impossible to refute as to sustain, for we are involved in a theological conundrum on which no completely satisfying light has been thrown. For, in speaking of bringing good out of evil, of creating being from nonbeing, the theologian is generally thinking of God's intervention by changing expected effects from causes through the miraculous or at least supernatural creation of new causes that modify existing effects. Thus Samson's heaven-gifted strength modifies the effects of Hebraic defeat, which we are given to understand that Hebraic sins well merited. Samson's sins contribute to a new intervention in cause and effect in the sense that his being a prisoner leads to the opportunity of inflicting universal catastrophe upon the Philistines. This last result, however, is not particularly satisfying to the reader unless he can respond to a spirit of vindictiveness. At least the Fall in *Paradise Lost* can be interpreted to mean an evolutionary gain in knowledge—at a price, of course—and the paradox of the Fortunate Fall has its consoling side. But Milton assumes the reader's hatred for the Philistines rather than artistically stimulating it as he did in the case of the devils in the epic.

The Greek tragedian met the paradox of good coming out of evil in the bleakest terms. The protagonist is damned if he does and damned if he doesn't. The gods demand that man avenge his father by killing his mother, but he will nevertheless be punished for killing his mother. He would also be punished for not killing his mother. Milton's version of Christianity offers a more complex way to meet such a paradox. It is assumed that it is right for Samson to destroy the Philistines (who paradoxically have also been God's instrument for chastising the Hebrews —in a sense they have been doing God's will but must be punished for it). It would be a sin for Samson to reject this vocation. He falters by doing a humane act—falling in love with Dalila (actually marrying her, according to Milton's innovation). It was wrong for him to falter according to the play; but would it not have been wrong for him not to falter? Milton indicates that Samson acts right when he acts as an agent of God, even when he does some rather horrible things; he acts wrong when he acts for himself, even when he acts rather decently. It is not to be supposed that God or the gods deliberately place Samson in this dilemma; it is he himself. Critics have asserted that the play emphasizes a strong Protestant sense of individual responsibility. Milton insists that Samson's evil is his own, and Samson accepts full responsibility for it:

> Nothing of these evils hath befall'n me
> But justly; I myself have brought them on,
> Sole Author I, sole cause. . . .
> (374–376)

On the other hand, the dilemma remains that it may have been

God's plan to use Samson's weakness in furthering his objective against the Philistines. Milton could argue, of course, that Samson's sin had already been discounted in the major computers of Providence, that Providence can bring good out of evil, can anticipate evil, but that personal sin had to be personally expiated.

There is little sense in this play of the mercy and compassion to which we are accustomed in the author of "Lycidas" and *Paradise Lost*. There is little of the great classical sense that mankind *means* all men. As in *Paradise Regained*, some hardness has entered Milton's view of people in the mass:

> Nor do I name of men the common rout,
> That wand'ring loose about
> Grow up and perish, as the summer fly,
> Heads without name no more remember'd
> But such as thou hast solemnly elected. . . .
> (674–678)

The concept of loving one's enemies, even in the sense of trying to understand them, was never excessively strong in Milton, either as a poet or as a pamphleteer. The chorus accepts the human disaster following the political catastrophe achieved by Samson with an almost irritating complacency:

> . . . Samson hath quit himself
> Like Samson, and heroicly hath finish'd
> A life Heroic, on his Enemies
> Fully reveng'd hath left them years of mourning,
> And lamentation to the Sons of Caphtor
> Through all Philistian bounds. . . .
> (1708–1713)

Even Providence, like the Greek *ate*, maintains a spirit of vindictiveness unrelieved by any disguise of humanistic grace:

Ideas in the Poems

> Along them hee a spirit of frenzy sent,
> Who hurt thir minds,
> And urg'd them on with mad desire
> To call in haste for thir destroyer. . . .
> (1675–1678)

But there is one strong humanizing element in *Samson Agonistes* that softens the somewhat harsh atmosphere of the work. Milton was brought up in the tradition of the medieval debate; it served him in good artistic stead. If Comus is thought by some critics to win a fair share of the argument, even more strongly can it be maintained that Milton goes out of his way for Dalila. Of course, there is no way to prove this conclusively—a great deal depends on the individual reader's feeling for the movement of the play. Without warrant from the scriptural history, Milton had made Dalila Samson's wife rather than his mistress. This change can be viewed in either of two lights: as an attempt to increase the moral dignity of Dalila or to increase even more the ingratitude of her treachery. She appears on stage, "With all her bravery on, and tackle trim, / Sails fill'd, and streamers waving . . ." (717–719). She weeps, "wetting the borders of her silk'n veil" (730). The chorus is antagonistic to her, but the image she presents of herself carries a certain conviction; at least in her own words there is no real hint of concealed hypocrisy:

> . . . But conjugal affection,
> Prevailing over fear and timorous doubt,
> Hath led me on desirous to behold
> Once more thy face, and know of thy estate.
> (739–742)

She argues that she acted as she did under the religious and patriotic gestures of her people and to keep Samson close to her and out of danger. Her fault, she claims, has risen out of weakness and out of love ("Love hath oft, well meaning, wrought much woe," 813). Samson responds rather curtly for a man who has felt so guilty about himself:

> All wickedness is weakness; that plea therefore
> With God or Man will gain thee no remission.
> (834–835)

Dalila argues from abstract political philosophy:

> ... to the public good
> Private respects must yield. ...
> (867–868)

And Samson responds in kind:

> ... if aught against my life
> Thy country sought of thee, it sought unjustly
> Against the law of nature, law of nations. ...
> (887–889)

In line with the antifeminine statements of the play, Dalila seems very apologetic about being a woman:

> First granting, as I do, it was a weakness
> In me, but incident to all our sex,
> Curiosity, inquisitive, importune
> Of secrets, then with like infirmity
> To publish them, both common female faults ...
> (773–777)

and

> In argument with men, a woman ever
> Goes by the worse, whatever be her cause.
> (903–904)

Samson pours scorn on her, somewhat forgetting his earlier contention that he was the sole author and the sole cause of his evils (374–376). This "hyaena" has an "adder's wisdom"—he will not be uxorious to her will in perfect thraldom (945–946). Dalila relieves all these abstract wranglings by an incarnational gesture—a human touch in a world of acrid theology and politics—"Let me approach at least, and touch thy hand" (951). But Samson will have none of it:

> Not for thy life, lest fierce remembrance wake
> My sudden rage to tear thee joint by joint.
> (952–953)

In reponse to the plea for forgiveness she had previously uttered, he answers ambiguously. He forgives in a purely *noli-me-tangere* way, and, in that sense, does not really forgive at all:

> At distance I forgive thee, go with that. . . .
> (954)

A dour atmosphere pervades the play—there is not much of "virtue in her shape how lovely" (*Paradise Lost* IV, 848). It is difficult to imagine how Samson could ever have been seductive or seducible.

If the atmosphere of *Samson Agonistes* marks a decline in Milton's humanistic approach and a reversal to Puritanism more in keeping with some of the spirit of the Old Testament, the form is deliberately and consciously classical.[27] Euripides is echoed in the opening soliloquy, with its characterization of Dalila and its chain of philosophical reasoning. The model of Sophocles can be found in the continuous use of dramatic irony, the subjection of the hero's will to a number of tests, the handling of the chorus, and the denouement. The drama's unity, the limitation of characters and plot, the self-control of the protagonist, the strong feeling for righteousness which flows throughout the drama are reminiscent of Aeschylus. The unities are observed;

the scene throughout the play is "before the prison in Gaza," and the action begins at sunrise and ends at dawn. Coleridge's assertion that *Samson Agonistes* is "the finest imitation of Greek drama that had been or ever would be written"[28] has been sympathetically reflected in other critics.

But, in spite of the sympathy of many critics, several notes that are not Hellenic distinguish *Samson Agonistes*. The medieval theme for tragedy—the fall from greatness—is more prominent than in the Greek plays:

> The rarer thy example stands,
> By how much from the top of wondrous glory,
> Strongest of mortal men,
> To lowest pitch of abject fortune thou art fall'n.
> (166–169)

There is no progression in Samson through the overweening self-confidence of *hybris* to the desperate extravagance of *ate* by which the hero destroys himself. Even that power which in Greek tragedy must remain inviolate participates in this reversal of fortune:

> Not only dost degrade them, or remit
> To life obscur'd, which were a fair dismission,
> But throw'st them lower than thou didst
>   exalt them high. . . .
> (687–689)

The traditional emotions of pity and fear are not aroused and resolved according to the classical formula. We may pity Samson's situation at the beginning, we may sympathize with his anger toward Dalila and the Philistines, but we cannot feel sorry for or fear for him at the end of the play, for the clear purpose of the drama is to show a climactic development from a low to a high spiritual estate—"nothing is here for tears" (1721). The

Ideas in the Poems

story of Samson is one of spiritual success in which no unresolved ambiguities are meant to remain. In Greek tragedy, the protagonist is defeated by powers that are conventionally understood to be just and yet whose justice on the operational level is questionable, certainly ambiguous.

It has been argued, with some validity, that *Samson Agonistes* presents, in place of a *catharsis*, a *lustratio*, a word implying "a religious purification." This is the term Milton himself uses in his prefatory material to the drama. According to Merritt Y. Hughes, Milton reflects the thought of Minturno in his *Arte Poetica* in thinking of tragedy as "agonistic," "a kind of spiritual athletic discipline like the hard physical training of the Spartans," which trains men to endure reversals of fortune.[29]

Though it has been asserted that Samson is a prototype of Christ,[30] and though there are undoubted overtones of this tradition in the drama, its spirit is markedly different from that of the Christ who prayed that this chalice would pass from him and who forgave his enemies, for they knew not what they did.

NOTES

[1] Robert Burton, *The Anatomy of Melancholy*, (London: G. Bell, 1927) II, 131.
[2] *Ibid.*, II, 143.
[3] *Ibid.*, II, 143.
[4] *Ibid.*, II, 138.
[5] *Ibid.*, II, 93.
[6] *Ibid.*, II, 132–137.
[7] *Ibid.*, III, 358 ff.
[8] *Ibid.*, III, 394.
[9] *Ibid.*, III, 485.
[10] Undoubtedly this respect hearkened back to the life of the medieval hermit, ("Find out the peaceful hermitage," "Il Penseroso," 168). Who would deny the hermit's weeds and maple dish? In Spenser we have the recurrent image of the hermit living the life of contemplation in the

great forest (he is sometimes the noble knight who has forsaken the aristocratic way for something higher):

> Thence forward by that painfull way they pas
> Forth to an hill that was both steepe and hy,
> On top whereof a sacred chappell was,
> And eke a little Hermitage thereby,
> Wherein an aged holy man did lie,
> That day and night said his devotion,
> Ne other world'ly business did apply:
> His name was hevenly Contemplation;
> Of God and goodnes was his meditation.
>
> (*The Faerie Queene* I, x, st. xlvi)

[11] Plato, *Symposium*, trans. Benjamin Jowett, in *The Works of Plato*, ed. Irwin Edman (New York, 1956) 378–379.

[12] Cf. Arthur S. P. Woodhouse, "Comus Once More," *University of Toronto Quarterly* XIX (1950) 218–223.

[13] Robert Martin Adams, *Ikon*, 9.

[14] Cf. E. M. W. Tillyard, "The Action of Comus," *Studies in Milton* (London, 1951) 82–89.

[15] For the light that Robert Burton's *Anatomy of Melancholy* throws on the Miltonic crux at the end of the anticlerical passage ("that two-handed engine at the door," line 130), see my article, "Notes on Robert Burton and John Milton," *Studies in Philology* LIII, No. 4 (October, 1955) 578–591.

[16] Northrop Frye, *Anatomy of Criticism: Four Essays* (Princeton, 1957) 121.

[17] William G. Madsen, "The Voice of Michael in 'Lycidas'" *Studies in English Literature, 1500–1900* (Rice University) III, No. 1 (Winter, 1963) 6.

[18] It is very probable that Milton felt obliged to write on the subject of the temptations of Christ because of the pressure of Puritan tradition, to which he was socially and contextually allied even if he transcended its limitations and whether his artistic inspiration was fully at work or not. William Haller in *The Rise of Puritanism*, p. 151, throws light on Milton's choice of subject in *Paradise Regained*: "The Puritan saga did not cherish the memory of Christ in the manger or on the cross, that is, of the lamb of God sacrificed in vicarious atonement for the sins of man. The mystic birth was the birth of the new man in men. The mystic passion was the crucifixion of the new man by the old, and the true propitiation was the sacrifice of the old to the new. Hence the preachers lavished their powers upon describing all existence and every human life as

Ideas in the Poems

a phase of conflict between Christ and Satan. The first scene was the encounter of the old man, Adam, with the new and greater man, Christ, the second Adam, in the wilderness, and the tempter's rebuff." If Haller's observation is correct, Milton is completing that second scene is *Paradise Regained.*

[19] Whether *Paradise Regained* should be classified as an epic as well as a narrative poem is a matter of opinion. It is not an epic in the full-fledged sense of the classical tradition, with a panoply of various conventions aiming at "instructive wonder." For a full background of "the brief biblical epic," see Barbara Kiefer Lewalski's *Milton's Brief Epic: The Genre, Meaning and Art of Paradise Regained* (Providence, 1966). Two major studies of the background of ideas entering the poem are Elizabeth Marie Pope's *Paradise Regained: The Tradition and the Poem* (New York, 1962) and Arnold Stein's *Heroic Knowledge* (Minneapolis, 1957).

[20] Elizabeth Marie Pope, *Paradise Regained: The Tradition and the Poem,* 13.

[21] James Holly Hanford, *John Milton, Englishman* (New York, 1949) 212.

[22] F. Michael Krouse, *Milton's Samson and the Christian Tradition* (Princeton, 1949) 54.

[23] *Ibid.,* 41.

[24] *Ibid.,* 17.

[25] Cf. Krouse, 37 ff.

[26] Arnold Stein, *Heroic Knowledge,* 205.

[27] Milton's indebtedness to classical models is fully explored in William Riley Parker's *Milton's Debt to Greek Tragedy in Samson Agonistes* (Baltimore, 1937).

[28] Samuel Taylor Coleridge, *Seven Lectures on Shakespeare and Milton,* ed. J. Payne Collier (London, 1856) xxvii.

[29] Merritt Y. Hughes, *John Milton: Complete Poems and Major Prose* (New York, 1957) 549, n. 3.

[30] T. S. K. Scott-Craig argues in "Concerning Milton's Samson," *Renaissance News* V, No. 3 (Autumn, 1952) 45–53, that "Milton regarded tragedy, and the tragedy of Samson in particular, as a lustration, as a symbolic form of ransoming, of deliverance, of redemption from fear" (48). In answer to the question of where is Milton's celebration of the atonement, Scott-Craig observes that "his celebration is his poem on the spiritual agony of Christ; though like a good Christian he treats the matter at a respectful distance, typologically; or as we would say today, in prototype. Samson Agonistes is really Christus Agonistes" (46).

VI

Milton as a Poet

GREEK literary style, as Edith Hamilton has pointed out, arises from a language full of delicately modifying words, capable of the finest distinctions of meaning, but literal, grave, unemphatic. Even Greek poetic imagery was realistic but impatient of detail. "Birds were birds but nothing else, but how beautiful a thing is a bird 'that flies over the foam of the wave with careless heart, sea-purple bird of spring.'"[1] Greek style is terse, succinct, intense. As Douglas Bush observes, "One pervasive element in classical art which devotees of metaphysical peculiarity cannot abide is its generalizing habit, its refusal to number the streaks of the tulip. In Milton, as in the ancients, that habit springs from the instinct for rendering the normal and the universal, not the peculiar. The result may appear 'simple,' but it is not thin."[2]

Milton's sense of surface form, particularly in "Lycidas" and *Samson Agonistes*, is Hellenic. But as a late Renaissance humanist he has been deeply influenced by Virgil, the Italian stylists, and, in a general way, by the atmosphere of baroque art (particularly in the latter's handling of spacial relationships). The language of Milton is so constructed that an initiated reader is constantly reminded of classical passages. Underlying the English statement and its own mental associations is the added pleasure of classical "recall." Milton's schooling had called for a close reading of the classical originals, which, in turn, had to be imitated according to severe and very clearly stated rhetorical laws. A humanistic education was not only scholarly; it involved a great deal of creative writing. The principle of imitation practiced in schools of the humanistic tradition (such as St. Paul's which Milton attended) was by no means mechanical. The "retractio" of the model, the new rendering, was meant to develop new skills and new creative insights which could be pleasurably compared with their initial sources. This practice correlates with what is considered the most honorable task a Renaissance poet could aspire to: to distill in a vernacular language as much as possible of the spirit of the great classical poets. Davis P. Harding says of Milton, "No English poet, perhaps no poet except Virgil, has ever cultivated with more assiduity the art of verbal integration, the art of coercing two or more passages from one or more authors into a kind of fruitful collaboration with one another."[3]

Milton's language, though dependent on his classical training, is used in an original way. A critic has spoken of his "corporeal" word out of which the poet shapes aesthetic reality. "Ramism and the forces which fed into it in the seventeenth century induced men to leap the aural structures of syntactical discursion in search of an objective, 'corporeal' status for the word itself, a status in which it would not be a dependent sign but an immediate creative entity."[4] This corporeal reality is associated with mingled textures, meanings arranged in depth, with subsurface controls rising to our awareness.

As a public poet, Milton may often appear on the surface to

make generalized and conventionalized statements. The generalized statement, if viewed in a sympathetic light, is the universal classical statement. As one critic has remarked in regard to *Paradise Lost*, the theme required "the purging of the personal, the trivial, the local, yet without the exclusion of the natural and the simple. The stage is too vast, the panorama of hell, heaven, earth. It is plain that the immediate, the local and the individual cannot be allowed to dominate the epic situation."[5] In regard to the use of convention, we must remember that this was what a contemporary audience demanded, though we must also keep in mind that they were accustomed to the sophisticated use of convention in a creative way. Another critic wisely notes that "when Milton sat down to write a poem about Edward King, he did not ask himself: 'What can I find to say about King?' but 'How does poetry require that such a subject be treated?' The notion that convention shows a lack of feeling, and that a poet attains 'sincerity' (which usually means articulate emotion) by disregarding it, is opposed to all the facts of literary experience and history."[6] John Crowe Ransom finds that one of the great charms of "Lycidas" lies in its conventionality.[7] In regard to Milton's images, Rosemond Tuve remarks, "It was not their genesis in a vanished time but their power to outlive change that commended the figure to Milton."[8]

The classical background, the use of convention, the role of public statement—particularly the habit of stating something universally recognized in a dignified way—have run into a good deal of hostility among contemporary critics. The future will have to determine whether Milton is temporarily the victim of a hostile fashion or whether critical taste, particularly in regard to poetry, is about to enter a break with the past comparable to the gulf existent between the art of the Renaissance and modern abstract art.

Bush succinctly points to the source of the opposition. "There is, we are told, only one real and vital kind of poetry, and it is not Milton's kind. That is . . . poetry which simultaneously embraces diverse planes of experience and is characterized by realistic immediacy, particularity, and complexity, by a fusion of thought and feeling, by the interplay of irony and wit, and by diction, syntax, and rhythms which belong to the genius of the common speech."[9] Robert Martin Adams remarks that the New Criticism (perhaps now somewhat aging) "after beating through the underbrush of the minor poems, has ventured at last to assert that *Paradise Lost* itself has some merit, if read in a perverse and limited way."[10] Sir Herbert Read says of Milton's thought that it "was a system apart from his poetic feeling . . . he did not think poetically but expounded his thought in verse."[11]

Complaints have been made against the "intrinsic deficiencies" of Milton's style and against the "extrinsic influence" of Milton's verse.[12] Milton is alleged to exhibit "a feeling for words rather than a capacity for feeling *through* words; we are often, in reading him, moved to comment that he is 'external' or that he 'works from the outside' "[13] "The whole movement of Milton's work is not expressive but mechanical and ritualistic: the pattern, the stylized gesture and movement, has no particular expressive work to do, but functions by rote, of its momentum, in the manner of a ritual."[14] The question of whether ritual cannot be most important and creative in certain forms of art is, of course, preempted in this type of criticism. It is this very ritual that C. S. Lewis exhalts as "the mimetic dance of all Christendom."[15]

Obviously when conflicts of criticism run this deep, critics hold very different values about the nature of poetry itself. Anne Davidson Perry, in *Milton's Epic Voice: The Narrator in Paradise Lost*, points to the source of the problem when she argues that the assumption that a poem "acts out" rather than "states" its meaning has dominated modern criticism and this assumption influences our preference for the kind of language that a poem should use "and our expectations about the way language should be organized."[16] We prefer, she claims, that kind of poetic imagery and diction which has sensuous immediacy and particularity, rather than abstractness and generality of statement. This attitude she connects with a distrust in systems of absolute values. "The distrust, whatever its causes, has so affected our critical judgments that many modern readers are no longer able to respond to literature of statement, suspecting it inevitably to be dogmatic or complacent or sentimental."[17]

The assumption seems to be that if the human condition is paradoxical, ambiguous, and open-ended, all and every kind of art should reflect this fact. Obviously, there is little chance of bridging the gap between this point of view and that of a poet uttering inspired truth under the guidance of the Holy Spirit. Poetry demands intuitive and affirmative statement (even an affirmative statement about negatives such as hatred, despair, frustration) rather than discursive demonstration, and, on the level of affirmation rather than argumentation, any *total* assent to the poet's ideas is not requisite for enjoying his poetry. Otherwise, the only poetry we could enjoy is that reflecting our own ideas. Is not all poetry dogmatic in an intuitive sense? When poetry is criticized for being dogmatic, is it not generally a criticism of manner rather than of content? As Adams shrewdly observes, "One does not seek agreement or disagreement with particular beliefs but an awareness of the feelings associated with holding them; one does not cherish specific, literal ideas, which may be true or false, alive or dead, coherent or incoherent, wicked or virtuous, but the fullness of an idea worked out as thoroughly and largely as may be."[18]

Milton as a Poet

Milton conceives of poetry as public statement observing classical decorum. It is only very incidentally a revelation of interior psychic conditions. It is a tendency in contemporary criticism to assume that the overt theme of a poem is far from being the real one. This has gone so far that a recent reactionary critic has been led to observe that a necessary condition for a competent reader of poetry is "a keen eye for the obvious."[19] Paul Elmer More a number of years ago cast doubt on "dissociation of sensibility," whereby, he alleges, each fact of sense experience is given, without discrimination, as an essential means for poetry.[20] Milton is not an artist open to any and every perception but only to those perceptions which suit the "decorum" and overall purpose of the work.

C. S. Lewis has declared that the disorganized consciousness which the modern critic may consider particularly real is, in fact, highly artificial. "It is discovered by introspection, that is, by artificially suspending all the normal and outgoing activities of the mind and then attending to what is left."[21] For Lewis, a work like the *Paradise Lost* is public *rite* and *ritual*. There is nothing private about it—not even Milton's remarks about his blindness at the beginning of Book III. It is the *office* of the blind bard that is sung, not the *person*.[22] The more ritual *Paradise Lost* becomes, Lewis argues "the more we are elevated to the rank of participants, precisely because the poet appears not as a private person but as a Hierophant or Choregus."[23] "We are summoned not to hear what one particular man thought and felt about the Fall, but to take part, under his leadership, in a great mimetic dance of all Christendom, ourselves soaring and ruining from Heaven, ourselves enacting Hell and Paradise, the Fall and the repentance."[24]

These are conservative views and may not make sufficiently sympathetic allowance for the stress on the unconscious mind that has pervaded much of modern art since the impact of Carl Jung and Sigmund Freud. Nevertheless, the point is well taken that if we can deceive ourselves by the conscious image we create and project while neglecting strong unconscious forces, we can also fall into the opposite error of accepting the expression of the unconscious as a total reality while neglecting traditional conscious forces. In any event, Milton means himself to be a public artist, his conscious mind always alert, always following the dedicated vocation of the artist in the high humanist tradition.

Should not a major poet have a certain kind of spiritual generosity or magnificence? We might possibly think also of austerity, sublimity. It is relevant to ask what Milton himself thinks. Milton uses the adjectives: *simple, sensuous, passionate*.[25] Great poetry certainly is not simple-minded, but must have that ultimate simplicity that is the end result of great intellectual concentration (*simple*). It must have emotional intensity, and especially the poet's vision must have not only immediate perception (*sensuous*) but sustained energy (*passion*). The "visionary gleam," as we call it, may not be sufficient in itself for a really sustained effort. And Milton makes massive efforts. He had to have a conviction about his vocation, about the high dignity of being a poet, about the idea of the poet as a great teacher, as a great citizen. All these values were necessary for his sustained effort, carried on through years of intensive work and physical disability.

The emotional response of every poet has individual characteristics. No two poets evoke in the same way. For example, Milton's response to nature is in terms of its more hidden, subtle forms. He thinks of such sights as "youthful Poets dream / On Summer eves by haunted stream," or he thinks of the moon that has been led astray "Through the Heav'n's wide pathless way." He thinks of the ocean, "Over some wide water'd shore /

Swinging slow with sullen roar." We always associate with Milton such images as the gray-hooded even, and the morn with sandals gray. The images are presented with extreme sensibility to their sounds and to the subdued subtleties of their colors. Milton's adjectives are applied with analytical skill, with that kind of classical emphasis which is entirely accurate and arrives at the essence of the thing described.

He sees in nature more than direct or obvious experience. He is aware (especially in his description of Paradise) of that sense of repose, the climactic pause in the activities of the day, bringing intuitions of peace, of presence, of benediction—for God is truly walking in the afternoon air. Often he thinks of the quiet and insistent song of the far-off planets, a harmony of familiar sounds that do not reach the gross ear but the ear that is reverent and attentive. He loves to describe the beauties of the English countryside, often for its own sake without other implications. He says:

> Sweet is the breath of morn, her rising sweet,
> With charm of earliest Birds; pleasant the Sun
> When first on this delightful Land he spreads
> His orient Beams, on herb, tree, fruit, and flow'r,
> Glist'ring with dew; fragrant the fertile earth
> After soft showers; and sweet the coming on
> Of grateful Ev'ning mild, then silent Night
> With this her solemn Bird, and this fair Moon
> And these the Gems of Heav'n, her starry train. . . .
> *(Paradise Lost* IV, 641–649)

This simple, instantaneous, but always perceptive reaction to natural beauty is a constant theme throughout his work and often relieves his more technical and intellectual discourse.

But the lyric poet of "still evening," of "twilight gray" and her "sober livery," yield to the public-spirited, grave, and passionate teacher in the trilogy of *Paradise Lost, Paradise Regained,* and *Samson Agonistes.* His basic idea of poetry is that of a public office performed in a disciplined and dedicated spirit. Milton himself expected a "fit audience, though few" (*Paradise Lost* VIII, 31). The tendency in contemporary education has been to make the Milton audience a small class of professional specialists, when what is really needed is the recruitment of numbers of intelligent and sensitive readers who are not necessarily literary specialists. If Milton is a difficult artist, it is not by reason of his articulation, for he took great pains to be precise and accurate. He is difficult only in the sense that he is the heir to rich traditions—classical, Hebraic, Christian—and deals with the profound and essential mysteries of human experience.

MILTON'S "HIGH" STYLE

While following wherever possible precedents established by tradition, Milton is aware that he is boldly handling difficult material on a scale which no one had yet tried. He is to undertake "Things unattempted yet in prose or rhyme" (*Paradise Lost* I, 16), and he recognizes the tremendous responsibility he has taken on. His invocation of the heavenly muse at the beginning of the epic is not merely conventional; it also symbolizes what was for him a humble and genuine necessity:

> . . . Thou from the first
> Wast present, and with mighty wings outspread
> Dove-like satst brooding on the vast Abyss
> And mad'st it pregnant. . . .
>
> (I, 19–22)

In calling on the aid of the heavenly muse for his adventurous song, he was fully conscious of what Renaissance aestheticians called the "high" style:

> That with no middle flight intends to soar
> Above th' Aonian Mount, while it pursues
> Things unattempted yet in Prose or Rhyme.
> (*Paradise Lost* I, 14–16)

This was the style suitable to his "higher argument" (*Paradise Lost* IX, 42). Though he wonders whether he is writing in an age too late (IX, 44), he must have a style commensurate with his theme:

> If answerable style I can obtain
> Of my Celestial Patroness....
> (*Paradise Lost* IX, 20–21)

Scaliger in his *Poetics* (1561) had distinguished three different styles of poetic utterance: the lofty, the humble, and the mean between these two (Book IV, ii). Common to all poetry are perspicuity, refinement, propriety, elegance or grace, and rhythm. "In the grand style those [qualities] to be observed always are dignity and sonorousness; those to be used on occasion, ponderousness [*gravitas*] and fervency [*vehementia*]."[26]

Edmund Spenser, without self-consciousness, adhered to the "second tenor," the mean between the two styles, as did Tasso and Ariosto. Spenser said he was going to mount to the "lofty style" in *The Faerie Queene* when Gloriana and her archenemy were to meet in final and decisive battle—a climax that was never written. Invoking the sacred muse, Spenser says:

> Fayre Goddesse, lay that furious fitt asyde,
> Till I of warres and bloody Mars doe sing,
> And Bryton fieldes with Sarazin blood bedyde,
> Twixt that great faery Queene and Paynim king,
> That with their horror heven and earth did ring;
> A worke of labour long, and endlesse prayse:
> But now a while lett downe that haughtie string,
> And to my tunes thy second tenor rayse,
> That I this man of God his godly armes may blaze.
> (*The Faerie Queene* I, xi, st. vii)

Milton rejected for his epic both the style and the subject matter that he had found in his beloved Spenser:

> Not sedulous by Nature to indite
> Wars, hitherto the only Argument
> Heroic deem'd, chief maistry to dissect
> With long and tedious havoc fabl'd Knights
> In Battles feign'd; the better fortitude
> Of Patience and Heroic Martyrdom
> Unsung; or to describe Races and Games,
> Or tilting Furniture, emblazon'd Shields,
> Impreses quaint, Caparisons and Steeds;
> Bases and tinsel Trappings, gorgeous Knights
> At Joust and Tournament. . . .
> (*Paradise Lost* IX, 27–37)

The high style, according to Scaliger, should possess dignity, sonorousness, and, where suitable, ponderousness and fervency. This is a succinct summary of the very qualities exhibited in *Paradise Lost*.

In regard to the technical accomplishment of his verse in his great epic, Milton more than met Scaliger's demand for sonorousness. His sonorousness is not just some calm and relaxing medium; it is infused with many striking kinds of energy. It would include nearly all the common properties of poetry which Scaliger listed as not invariably used but subject to occasion: smoothness (*mollitia*), winsomeness (*suavitas*), rapidity of spirit (*incitatio*), purity or unadornedness (*puritas*), acumen (*acutum*), sharpness or raillery (*acre*), fullness (*plenum*), and ornateness (*floridum*).

Sometimes Milton's sonority is that of the sullen roar of the ocean, which he mentioned in "Il Penseroso." Above all the waves, eddies, and currents is the vast harmony of the ocean that also embraces cacophony. The background rhythm continues its steady reconciliation of opposites at all times, but the immediate rhythm breaks upon the beach irregularly, while the mounting waves behind may follow almost instantly, or there may be an interval of mounting calm, or a vast movement suddenly cut off, left deserted in the steady hum of a wine-dark sea. E. M. W. Tillyard remarks that "he refuses to measure out the sentences of his rhythms in doublets. He must prolong his sentences with subordinate and participial clauses till they are ripe to dropping and he will not relinquish his rhythms until they have worked themselves out to exhaustion and rest."[27] An English poet, Laurence Binyon, once observed: "Indeed it is a continuity of sustained rhythm, sustained not only by the drawn-out harmonies of sound but by the momentum of intellectual energy within them, so that we seem as if borne onward over an ocean out of sight of land. It is this which above all else is Milton's."[28] Images drawn from movements of the ocean seem to be almost the only way to offer an analogy for Milton's rhythmic effects.

Harding notes that Milton's verse paragraph is modeled on Virgil's, with less serenity but more rough power: "This is Virgil's verse paragraph, but with a difference, for Milton has not only succeeded in achieving Virgil's rhythmic span, he has remarkably extended its limits."[29] Another commentator argues that Milton achieved the magnificence of the heroic style that was the aim of Italian humanism—the *asprezza* (difficulty) of the *versi sciolti* (blank verse). An Italian humanist speaks of the marvelous beauty of this kind of poetry, even better comprehended by the mind than by the ear, "colored not, so to speak, with artificial enamel, but with its own natural blood."[30] It was the Italian Renaissance view that if blank verse were to succeed, it must be largely by virtue of a special power and beauty of diction. Consensus among traditionalists has held that Milton abundantly supplied them.

Ideas in Milton

MILTON'S POETRY AND THE BAROQUE

The sense of space, of spacial grandeur, in Milton has been attributed in part, by Marjorie Nicolson and others, to the scientific discoveries of the seventeenth century, particularly those of Galileo. Milton was deeply interested in the new astronomy, as the long discussion between Adam and Raphael indicates in Book VIII of *Paradise Lost*. In tribute to the scientist Milton creates a great image that has a kind of moonlit resonance with its sonorous Italian place names:

> . . . the broad circumference
> Hung on his shoulders like the Moon, whose Orb
> Through Optic Glass the Tuscan Artist views
> At Ev'ning from the top of Fesole,
> Or in Valdarno, to descry new Lands,
> Rivers or Mountains in her spotty Globe.
> (*Paradise Lost* I, 286–291)

Here is exactly the right synthesis of suggestions of solitude, mystery, adventure, and, above all, the appropriate serenity. He suggests not only scientific space but—what is more important—psychological space.

Milton succeeds in capturing dramatic land- and seascapes on a kind of mental microfilm. This is true whether he is presenting the still evening gray with its distant music in *Comus*, the destructive violence of the sea in its mad washings from the Hebrides to Michael's Mount in "Lycidas," or Satan's journey through Chaos. The imagery is hard and crisp; there is no blurring of focus.

Such images, in the main, are due to Milton's distinctive genius, but they also mark one of his several indebtednesses to baroque art. The baroque can be considered as an artistic method independently of its being symbolic of a specific cultural attitude. Though Milton at times shares its attitudes, he is always adept at using its techniques.

The baroque is related to the classical rather than opposed to it. A main distinction, which explains the attraction of the baroque for the mystics and religious poets of the seventeenth century, is that in classical art the moment is arrested and immortalized, whereas in baroque art the moment is still fluid, caught in a tide of unappeasable yearning. Keats, in his "Ode to a Grecian Urn," defined the classical spirit extremely well—the lover cannot approach his goal, but he and his love will be forever fair, "breathing human passion far above." Classical art, though intensely alive within the terms of the concrete epiphany, has a monumental air. Baroque art creates a psychological illusion of a very different kind. It expresses an aspiration and emotional drive in which both time and eternity are beheld *now* in dynamic surge, and yet a mysterious (in this sense almost classical) control is maintained over these dynamisms. Baroque art is warmer than the classical, more concerned with the relationship of persons, more concerned in pressing the borders of reality to attain its goal.

This psychological effect arises from a certain way of using spacial relationships. The high achievement of baroque architecture was to enclose space while at the same time suggesting freedom unlimited within the confines of stone and mortar. The actual cosmology of *Paradise Lost* in itself would not serve this purpose any better than raw bricks. Milton, as a baroque architect, constructs space that is free and apparently unconfined but not limitless or chaotic. The paradox is achieved by a balance of dynamisms—one outward and one returning. "Lycidas" offers in a nutshell what Milton carries out on a vast scale in *Paradise Lost*. The water imagery of the poem constantly suggests the unlimited ("wizard stream"; "down the swift Hebrus"; "under the whelming tide"). Yet the vast water world is circumscribed, for all its uncircumscribed movements, by the idea of home ("Look homeward Angel now"), the point to which the dynamisms return. Just as the baroque church is utterly free and yet intimately the *house* of God, so are Milton's vast oceans drawn in reverse movement by the compelling magnetism of *homeward*:

> ... Whilst thee the shores and sounding Seas
> Wash far away, where'er thy bones are hurl'd,
> Whether beyond the stormy Hebrides
> Where thou perhaps under the whelming tide
> Visit'st the bottom of the monstrous world;
> Or whether thou to our moist vows denied,
> Sleep'st by the fable of Bellerus old,
> Where the great vision of the guarded Mount
> Looks toward Namancos and Bayona's hold;
> Look homeward Angel now....
> (154–163)

In all the great conflicts, tragic ironies, cosmic travels of *Paradise Lost* we move, as in "Lycidas," to the climax of the quiet return:

> ... then wilt thou not be loath
> To leave this Paradise, but shalt possess
> A paradise within thee, happier far.
> (*Paradise Lost* XII, 585–587)

> The World was all before them, where to choose
> Thir place of rest, and Providence thir guide....
> (*Paradise Lost* XII, 646–647)

The search for endlessness, even the endlessness of the ego—if not presented under tragic terms as in the case of Satan—can be boring, for it violates the sense of organic growth, of climax, of epiphany, suitable to a human being. The fact is that the idea of infinity, whether of space or time, can be psychologically dull unless it is brought into a human relationship that deepens and inspires. Man is only briefly impressed by size. Alexander Pope's observation of man—"his time a moment, and a point his space"—is depressing, and hardly anyone believes it, because it is psychologically so inadequate. The late G. K. Chesterton had a profound intuition about man's reaction to size: "When one is fond of anything one addresses it by diminutives. . . . The reason is, that anything, however huge, that can be conceived of as complete, can be conceived of as small."[31] The baroque could embrace the limitless and conceive of it as a whole (without losing its many-dimensional dynamism) and guide it back incarnationally to the house, the home.

It is needless to belabor the thesis that Milton had the temperament and the technique for the highest baroque art. What is not quite so obvious is that he also shared some of the ideology and mental preoccupations with which baroque art in the seventeenth century was chiefly concerned.

It may be because Milton has been so closely associated with the Protestant tradition that the word *baroque* has not been freely applied to him. Baroque art has generally been associated with the Counter-Reformation. One of Catholicism's reactions to the simplicity and austerity of the Reformed Church was an almost grandiloquent display of aesthetic forms. An interesting contrast can be made between the architecture of Protestant Wittenberg in Saxony and that of Catholic Salzburg in Austria; the one was severe to the point of drabness; the other even had putti and heraldic forms on the bishop's stables. Though, undeniably, baroque art is closely associated with a revived Catholicism, it also affected in very definite ways Protestant artists, particularly literary artists.

Exuberance does not have to be baroque, but the baroque artistic method was the normal means of expressing emotion in the seventeenth century. In this respect, we have to move from Milton's "Puritan" image to the fact of his exuberance. Wylie Sypher states in *The Four Stages of Renaissance Style* that Milton had an exuberant baroque delight in the power of the material.[32] Tillyard in *The Miltonic Setting* remarks "It was Saurat, I believe, who first pointed out the feeling that Milton had for fertility, for exuberant life. . . . It is a simple and common feeling but Milton had it with a force quite exceptional even among poets, as if his own teeming brain and soaring temperament were in some intimate way linked with the apparent lavishness of nature in perpetuating the forms of life."[33]

Baroque art had a special way of emphasizing imagistic expression, which is certainly basic to poetry. St. Ignatius Loyola in his *Spiritual Exercises* particularly stressed the use of the senses as a means of knowing and of higher contemplation. This tradition was not entirely new with St. Ignatius, but he gave it special emphasis. We meditate on Christ, perhaps on his sufferings, his actual wounds, and from these sense impressions we move on to more abstract and universal considerations. This discipline can, of course, break down at that point where the individual is content merely with the images (as in some modern poetry) and loses sight of the great transcendent unity to which these specific things should point. We may reverence St. Peter's rather than St. Peter himself. The main aim of the baroque was to make vivid and to dramatize sense impressions as strong foundations and as starting-off points for the highest contemplation.

"L'Allegro" and "Il Penseroso" are the two poems of Milton that verbalize baroque concepts most directly, though they have nothing like the great baroque insights of "Lycidas" and *Paradise Lost*. The baroque movement had been given further stress and strength by the Spanish mystics, and certain key seventeenth-century words, particularly *ecstasy*, are connected with that tradition. Meditation, contemplation, ecstasy are deepening stages of a spiritual experience—thinking about, actually beholding, being transported into. Milton could already have found in Shakespeare and Robert Burton the concept of meditation as a power moving swiftly to seize reality. Hamlet had responded to his supernatural visitant in words that are normally rather difficult to explain in the classroom:

> Haste me to know't, that I, *with wings as swift*
> *As meditation* or the thoughts of love,
> May sweep to my revenge.
> (*Hamlet* I, v, 29–31)

Meditation partakes of wisdom, with which it can be partially identified, and wisdom is more active than all active things. Robert Burton's *Anatomy of Melancholy* points out the relationship of meditation to contemplation, emphasizing their speed of movement. He quotes St. Augustine in regard to the beauty of God: *make clean thine heart, purify thine heart, if thou wilt see this beauty, prepare thyself for it.* Burton then adds: "*It is the eye of contemplation, by which we must behold it, the wing of meditation which lifts us up and rears our souls with the motion of our hearts, and sweetness of contemplation: so saith Gregory*, cited by Bonaventure. And as *Philo Judaeus* seconds him, *He that loves God will soar aloft and take him wings.* . . ."[34]

Milton calls upon Contemplation in "Il Penseroso" as a "pensive Nun, devout and pure" (31), and we come close to the image of a Spanish painting, such as an El Greco, a picture of a saint whose eyes are rapt heavenward (and yet in a reverse movement return to earth):

> Come, but keep thy wonted state,
> With ev'n step, and musing gait,
> And looks commercing with the skies,

> Thy rapt soul sitting in thine eyes:
> There held in holy passion still,
> Forget thyself to Marble, till
> With a sad Leaden downward cast,
> Thou fix them on the ground as fast.
> ("Il Penseroso" 37–44)

Besides this central baroque image, there is an extensive vocabulary in the companion pieces of "L'Allegro" and "Il Penseroso" continually calling to mind the baroque. The passage at the end of "Il Penseroso" indicates a church that never characterized a Puritan environment but would admirably suit a baroque one:

> With antic Pillars massy proof,
> and storied Windows richly dight
> Casting a dim religious light.
> (158–160)

It is hardly necessary to stress the remaining vocabulary of the passage as strictly baroque in the highest sense, particularly in the association of "ecstasies" with "Heav'n."

> There let the pealing Organ blow
> To the full voic'd Choir below,
> In Service high and Anthems clear,
> As may with sweetness, through mine ear,
> Dissolve me into ecstasies,
> And bring all Heav'n before mine eyes.
> (161–166)

Exuberance certainly characterizes the following passage in "L'Allegro." The adjectives *wanton, giddy, melting* and the noun *mazes* are revealing, especially if our image of a Puritan is that of a person in almost exaggerated control of his feelings:

> Lap me in soft Lydian Airs,
> Married to immortal verse,

Such as the meeting soul may pierce
In notes, with many a winding bout
Of linked sweetness long drawn out,
With wanton heed, and giddy cunning,
The melting voice through mazes running;
Untwisting all the chains that tie
The hidden soul of harmony. . . .
(136–144)

NOTES

[1] Edith Hamilton, *The Greek Way to Western Civilization* (New York, 1963) 50.

[2] Douglas Bush, *Paradise Lost in Our Time* (Ithaca, N. Y., 1945) 93.

[3] Davis P. Harding, *The Club of Hercules: Studies in the Classical Background of Paradise Lost* (Urbana, Ill., 1962) 96.

[4] Jackson I. Cope, *The Metaphoric Structure of Paradise Lost* (Baltimore, 1962) 178.

[5] Arnold Stein, *Answerable Style: Essays on Paradise Lost* (Minneapolis, 1953) 122.

[6] Northrop Frye, *Anatomy of Criticism*, 97.

[7] Cf. John Crowe Ransom, "A Poem Nearly Anonymous," *The World's Body* (New York, 1938) 1–28. While Ransom points out that Milton was "not infected with our gross modern concept of 'originality,'" and that his work becomes the climax of a tradition, he was also brilliant and insubordinate.

[8] Rosemond Tuve, *Images and Themes in Five Poems by Milton* (Cambridge, 1957) 9.

[9] Douglas Bush, *Paradise Lost in Our Time*, 89.

[10] Robert Martin Adams, *Ikon*, 179.

[11] Sir Herbert Read, *Collected Essays* (London, 1938) 84.

[12] James Thorpe, "A Brief History of Milton Criticism," *Milton Criticism* (New York, 1950) 18.

[13] Cf. remarks of Bernard Bergonzi in "Criticism and the Milton Controversy," in *The Living Milton*, ed. Frank Kermode (London, 1960) 167, regarding the thought expressed by F. R. Leavis in *Revaluation* (London, 1936).

[14] Bergonzi, op. cit., 166–167.
[15] C. S. Lewis, A Preface to Paradise Lost, 59.
[16] Anne Davidson Perry, Milton's Epic Voice: The Narrator in Paradise Lost (Cambridge, 1963) 10.
[17] Ibid., 11.
[18] Robert Martin Adams, Ikon, 218.
[19] M. H. Abrams, "Five Types of Lycidas," in Milton's Lycidas: The Tradition and the Poem, ed. C. A. Patrides (New York, 1961) 231.
[20] Cf. Paul Elmer More, "How to Read 'Lycidas,'" On Being Human (Princeton, 1936) 184–202.
[21] C. S. Lewis, A Preface to Paradise Lost, 131.
[22] Ibid., 58.
[23] Ibid., 59.
[24] Ibid.
[25] Of Education, Complete Prose II, 403.
[26] Cf. The Great Critics, ed. James Harry Smith and Edd Winfield Parks (New York, 1951) 162.
[27] E. M. W. Tillyard, The Miltonic Setting: Past and Present (New York, 1938) 71.
[28] Laurence Binyon, "A Note on Milton's Imagery and Rhythm," in Seventeenth Century Studies (Oxford, 1938) 190.
[29] Davis P. Harding, The Club of Hercules, 126.
[30] F. T. Prince, The Italian Elements in Milton's Verse (Oxford, 1954) 54.
[31] G. K. Chesterton, Orthodoxy (London, 1908) 114.
[32] Wylie Sypher, The Four Stages of Renaissance Style (New York, 1956) 198.
[33] E. M. W. Tillyard, The Miltonic Setting, 69.
[34] Robert Burton, Anatomy of Melancholy, Part III, Sect. IV, Mem. I, Subs. I (London: G. Bell, 1927) III, 364.

EPILOGUE

WHY DO we keep going back to a great artist? Whether or not Milton is a monument to dead ideas, Miltonic criticism—even when it has a negative aspect—is today more alive, more perceptive in depth, more excited about Milton than ever in the past. We go to a great artist, not because he has answered everything or even because he has answered so much, but because he has been deeply concerned about the essential matters that are always at the back of our minds, however distracted we may be by the claims of immediate pressures. The direct facing of what is eternal in the life of man through the incarnational aspect of the present moment (for an artist must wed his awareness of "his time a moment, and a point his space" with what is genuinely transcendent) lies too deep in a major work of art to be "updated."

Man cannot look transcendently at transcendence; he must see it through his physical eyesight, his nervous system, the impact of the daily routine, and even the amount of sleep he has had. In short, an artist is a man and not an angel. But his intuitive powers have something angelic about them—something that goes beyond the present moment in which they are and must be exercised. Alexander Pope, the most polished of second-rate thinkers, once asked, with his customary innocence, "Or can a part contain the whole?" The obvious answer is no, in a physical sense. But in a spiritual sense the answer is yes. The paradox of man is that he cannot empty the ocean into a cup, but, on the other hand, his intelligence can reach up to God himself.

Each man in each generation must seek to rediscover the great primal intuitions, so that they are not merely apprehended but comprehended, so that they are not merely on the surface of his awareness but become truly part of himself. An artist like Milton is a catalyst toward the re-creation in ourselves of such intuitions. In our age the Puritan ethos has largely run its course —and (more regretfully) the classical ethos as well. But Milton stands forth from his background like "an isolated volcano thrusting up through the philosophic plains, and drawing . . . fire from deeper and older [archetypal] levels of spiritual energy."[1] Each generation must honestly react to the artist in its own way (not necessarily the best way, and certainly not the last way). As for ourselves as critics, we must remain humble, however sharp we may be, for all criticism is incomplete. Arnold Stein reminds us, "One may make a definite study of all the known facts, but not a definite study of the meaning or beauty of a work of art."[2] The work of art remains constant, forever irradiating; it is we critics who must necessarily (and wisely) fluctuate.

Our world has, in its atomic competition, emulated Eve at her worst moment ("But keep the odds of Knowledge in my power," *Paradise Lost* IX, 820), but Milton, as Tillyard remarked, went in awe of the solemn terms on which life is lived on this earth.[3]

Epilogue

He had a sense of covenant, of the deep relationship of man to an eternal present. He did attain "To something like Prophetic strain"—not in the crass sense of foretelling future contingency, but in the sense of alerting us to the eternal present of God. A certain provincialism exists today, even among intellectuals and scholars, whereby those questions that have traditionally seemed the most important are regarded as increasingly irrelevant because there is no easy way to manipulate them in a scientific age by scientific method. The sensitive criticism which of recent years has been expended on Milton has done much to reduce the effect of this provincialism in regard to the appreciation of Milton's work. Milton has increasingly appeared as a much more complex and benign person than was once thought. Not, of course, that there should be a cult of perfectionism about him. In fact, the greater the artist, the more the imperfections become visible. It is not the perfection, but the energy and resources displayed in seeking perfection that distinguish greatness here. Great art, whether *Paradise Lost*, *Hamlet*, or *The Brothers Karamazov*, is not perfection but a massive and noble effort in human understanding. Milton did a disservice to himself in speaking of a fit audience, though few; his work is of such stature that it should be placed before all intelligent readers rather than being restricted to literary specialists.

A great artist must be read with the proper sense of space and of leisured timing. A general moral statement without space and context is simply a cliché. We have all heard them hundreds of times without conviction. Such statements only have power through a context that shows their foundations in the time and space of an artist's experience and to which we take the time and space to respond. As one philosopher has observed of Plato, "One can put the philosophy of Plato into a pamphlet, but it will not be the philosophy of Plato, because every important thought needs time and space for its display. One can compress the life of man, its significant events, into two days—yes, two days—but a man's few significant situations want around them many years, the full space of a whole life."[4]

Milton has repeatedly been called a nonconformist, but, as Peter Viereck once observed, "The meaningful moral choice is not between conforming and non-conforming, but between conforming to the ephemeral, stereotyped values of the moment and conforming to the ancient, lasting archetypal values shared by all creative cultures."[5] Milton expresses his dislike of outward conformity in a great variety of contexts. "Truth," he says, "is compared in Scripture to a streaming fountain; if her waters flow not in a perpetual procession, they sicken into a muddy pool of conformity and traditions."[6] He associates the cessation of knowledge with an obedient unanimity—"what a fine conformity would it starch us all into."[7] Though Milton has limitations, which are part of his time and part of the man, even in his nonconformity and even when his Puritanism reaches the most melancholy shades, his main bent always remains affirmative and creative. While many of us would disagree with numerous aspects of Miltonic theology and in spite his outbursts of "righteous" indignation, Milton has something of the spirit of ecumenism. He certainly conceives of the church as a living existential organism, charitable to a plurality of opinions, placing the spirit of the law above the letter, though we may consider him unrealistic in his rejection of institutions. He aims for universality, and, although it has been argued that he brings a rationalistic bent of mind to bear on the mysteries of life and religion, he bows before the wondrous and incomprehensible, seeing that in so far as reality is opaque, it is so not merely because of the limitations of human perception but because reality offers light within light, ever more dazzling. Sometimes, like the divine melancholy of contemplation itself, its bright visage has to be

Epilogue

"O'erlaid with black, staid Wisdom's hue,"[8] in order to adjust to the weaker gaze of mortals, "to hit the Sense of human sight."[9] For Milton, as for most mature men, there remain secrets that should be admired rather than scanned, and Milton did not hesitate to scan.

Milton's mind, like the minds of many great men, concentrated on a few driving ideas which he held with great intensity. His concepts of freedom, of civic duty, of the great bond between God and man; his sense that virtue has creative power (not merely fortitude); the imperative necessity he felt to master and embrace the energies of time, "the subtle thief of youth," by a life led on the highest level in terms of the great bond, the great covenant: to these values he gives the witness of passion and creative imagery, maintained through years of hard work, and, ultimately, through a crushing physical disability. But even more significant than the image of the intellectual searcher is the image of the man physically blind who could see spiritually what others could not:

> Blind Thamyris and blind Maeonides,
> And Tiresias and Phineus Prophets old.
> (*Paradise Lost* III, 35–36)

NOTES

[1] Basil Willey, *The Seventeenth Century Background*, 226.
[2] Arnold Stein, *Heroic Knowledge*, vii.
[3] E. M. W. Tillyard, *Studies in Milton*, 3.
[4] Max Picard in a letter to Henry Regnery, July 17, 1948.
[5] "The Unadjusted Man," *Saturday Review of Literature*, November 1, 1958.
[6] *Areopagitica*, *Complete Prose*, II, 543.
[7] *Ibid.*, 545.
[8] "Il Penseroso," line 16.
[9] *Ibid.*, line 14.

BIBLIOGRAPHY

Adams, Robert Martin. *Ikon: John Milton and the Modern Critics.* Ithaca: Cornell University Press, 1955.

Ames, Russell. *Citizen Thomas More and His Utopia.* Princeton: Princeton University Press, 1949.

Aristotle. *Basic Works*; trans. Richard McKeon. New York: Random House, 1941.

St. Augustine. *City of God*; trans. John Healey. 2 vols. Edinburgh: John Grant, 1909.

──────. *Confessions*; trans. Frank Sheed. New York: Sheed & Ward, 1943.

Barker, Arthur E. *Milton and the Puritan Dilemma, 1641–1660.* Toronto: University of Toronto Press, 1942.

Boethius. *The Consolation of Philosophy.* New York: Random House, 1943.

Bowra, C. M. *The Greek Experience.* New York: New American Library, 1961.

Burton, Robert. *The Anatomy of Melancholy.* 3 vols. London: G. Bell, 1937.

Bush, Douglas. *Paradise Lost in Our Time: Some Comments.* Ithaca: Cornell University Press, 1945.

Chambers, R. W. *Thomas More.* New York: Harcourt Brace, 1935.

Bibliography

Cope, Jackson I. *The Metaphoric Structure of Paradise Lost.* Baltimore: Johns Hopkins University Press, 1962.

Daiches, David. *Milton.* London: Hutchinson's Universal Library, 1957.

D'Arcy, M. C., S.J. *The Mind and Heart of Love: Lion and Unicorn, A Study in Eros and Agape.* New York: Henry Holt, 1947.

Dawson, Christopher. *Medieval Religion.* New York: Sheed & Ward, 1934.

Diekhoff, John S. *Milton's Paradise Lost.* New York: Humanities Press, 1958.

Empson, William. *Milton's God.* New York: New Directions, 1961.

Frye, Northrop. *Anatomy of Criticism: Four Essays.* Princeton: Princeton University Press, 1957.

_____. *The Return of Eden: Five Essays on Milton's Epics.* Toronto: University of Toronto Press, 1965.

Gilbert, Allan H. *On the Composition of Paradise Lost.* Chapel Hill: University of North Carolina Press, 1947.

Gilson, Etienne. *The Mystical Theology of Saint Bernard.* New York: Sheed & Ward, 1940.

Haller, William. *The Rise of Puritanism.* New York: Columbia University Press, 1938.

Hamilton, Edith. *The Greek Way to Western Civilization.* New York: New American Library, 1963.

Hanford, James Holly. *John Milton, Englishman.* New York: Crown, 1949.

Harding, Davis P. *The Club of Hercules: Studies in the Classical Background of Paradise Lost.* Urbana: The University of Illinois Press, 1962.

Kelley, Maurice. *This Great Argument: A Study of Milton's De Doctrina Christiana as a Gloss upon Paradise Lost.* Gloucester, Mass.: Peter Smith, 1962.

Kermode, Frank (ed.). *The Living Milton.* London: Routledge and Kegan Paul, 1960.

Krouse, F. Michael. *Milton's Samson and the Christian Tradition.* Princeton: Princeton University Press, 1949.

Lewalski, Barbara Kiefer. *Milton's Brief Epic: The Genre, Meaning* and Art of Paradise Regained. Providence: Brown University Press, 1966.

Lewis, C. S. A Preface to Paradise Lost. London: Oxford University Press, 1942.

Lovejoy, A. O. The Great Chain of Being. Cambridge: Harvard University Press, 1936.

Madsen, William G. "The Ideas of Nature in Milton's Poetry" in Three Studies in the Renaissance: Sidney, Jonson, Milton. New Haven: Yale University Press, 1958.

Marilla, E. L. The Central Problem of Paradise Lost: The Fall of Man. Cambridge, Harvard University Press, 1953.

Martz, Louis L. The Paradise Within: Studies in Vaughan, Traherne, and Milton. New Haven, Yale University Press, 1964.

_____. The Poetry of Meditation: A Study in English Religious Literature of the Seventeenth Century. New Haven: Yale University Press, 1954.

More, Paul Elmer. On Being Human. Princeton: Princeton University Press, 1936.

More, Sir Thomas. Utopia; trans. H. S. V. Ogden. New York: Appleton-Century Crofts, 1949.

Parker, William Riley. Milton's Debt to Greek Tragedy in Samson Agonistes. Baltimore: Johns Hopkins University Press, 1937.

Pater, Walter. The Renaissance. London: Macmillian, 1913.

Perry, Anne Davidson. Milton's Epic Voice: The Narrator in Paradise Lost. Cambridge: Harvard University Press, 1963.

Plato. The Republic; trans. Benjamin Jowett. New York: Colonial Press, 1901.

_____. Symposium; trans. Benjamin Jowett, in Works of Plato. ed. Irwin Edman. New York: Random House, 1956.

Pope, Elizabeth Marie. Paradise Regained: The Tradition and the Poem. New York: Russell & Russell, 1962.

Prince, F. T. The Italian Elements in Milton's Verse. Oxford: Clarendon Press, 1954.

Rajan, B. Paradise Lost and the Seventeenth Century Reader. London: Chatto & Windus, 1947.

Raleigh, Sir Walter. Milton. London: E. Arnold, 1900.

Roeder, Ralph. Man of the Renaissance. New York: Viking Press, 1933.

Bibliography

Samuel, Irene. *Dante and Milton: The Commedia and Paradise Lost*. Ithaca: Cornell University Press, 1966.

Saurat, Denis. *Milton: Man and Thinker*. London: Archon Books, 1964.

Stein, Arnold. *Answerable Style: Essays on Paradise Lost*. Minneapolis: University of Minnesota Press, 1953.

_____. *Heroic Knowledge*. Minneapolis: University of Minnesota Press, 1957.

Sypher, Wylie. *The Four Stages of Renaissance Style*. Garden City, N. Y.: Doubleday, 1955.

Thorpe, James (ed.). *Milton Criticism*. New York: Rinehart, 1950.

Tillyard, E. M. W. *Milton*. London: Chatto & Windus, 1949.

_____. *The Miltonic Setting: Past and Present*. New York: Macmillan, 1938.

_____. *Studies in Milton*. London: Chatto & Windus, 1951.

Tuve, Rosemund. *Images and Themes in Five Poems by Milton*. Cambridge: Harvard University Press, 1957.

Waldock, A. J. A. *Paradise Lost and Its Critics*. Gloucester, Mass.: Peter Smith, 1959.

Werblowsky, R. J. Zwi. *Lucifer and Prometheus: A Study of Milton's Satan*. London: Routledge, 1952.

Willey, Basil. *The Seventeenth Century Background*. London: Chatto & Windus, 1946.

ARTICLES

Bell, Millicent. "The Fallacy of the Fall," *PMLA* 68 (September, 1953) 863–883.

Grace, William J. "Notes on Robert Burton and John Milton," *Studies in Philology* LII, No. 4 (October, 1955) 578–591.

Greene, Clarence E. "The Paradox of the Fall in *Paradise Lost*," *Modern Language Notes* LIII (December, 1938) 557–571.

Madsen, William G. "The Voice of Michael in 'Lycidas,' " *Studies in English Literature, 1500–1900* (Rice University) III (Winter, 1963) 1–7.

Woodhouse, Arthur S. P. "Comus Once More," *University of Toronto Quarterly* XIX (1950) 218–223.

INDEX

Abrams, M. H., 173, 188 (n. 19)
Adam, 5, 21, 50, 63, 64
   relationship of Eve and, 72–75
   Samson as another, 152
Adams, Robert Martin, 37–38, 44, 68 (n. 20), 69 (n. 27), 136, 166 (n. 13), 171, 172, 187 (n. 10), 188 (n. 18)
Aeschylus, 163
Ames, Russell, 30 (n. 10)
Anatomy of Melancholy, 64, 71 (n. 65), 126–129, 165 (nn. 1–9), 166 (n. 15), 185, 188 (n. 34)
Apology Against a Modest Confutation, An, 16
Aquinas, St. Thomas
   on the active intelligence, 48–49
   meaning of grace in, 5
   meaning of nature in, 3–5
   Spenser better teacher than, 58
   thought compared with Milton's, 60–61
Areopagitica, 17–18, 31, (n. 21), 70 (n. 49), 81, 82, 83, 85, 99 (nn. 5–6), 192, 193 (n. 6)
Ariosto, Lodovico, 177

Aristotle, 62
Arminius, Jacobus, 6
Ascham, Roger, 48
Astraea, 40–41
Augustine, St., 2–3, 22, 29 (nn. 1–4), 31 (n. 22), 122 (n. 1), 155
   City of God, 2–3, 22, 31 (n. 22), 104, 105, 155
   Confessions, 104, 122 (n. 1)
   on meaning of nature, 3
   on original sin, 2
Augustinians, Late
   and illumination, 8
   and primacy of will, 51
Augustus, Caesar, 40

Bacon, Francis, 59
Barker, Arthur, 26, 31 (n. 33)
Belloc, Hilaire, 51, 70 (n. 42)
Bergonzi, Bernard, 187 (n. 13), 188 (n. 14)
Bernard of Clairvaux, St., 54–55
Binyon, Laurence, 179, 188 (n. 28)
Blake, William, 117
Boethius, 67, 71 (n. 69)
Borgia, Caesar, 9
Bowra, C. M., 66, 71 (n. 68)
Brothers Karamazov, The, 191

Burton, Robert, 64, 185
  See also Anatomy of Melancholy
Bush, Douglas, 46–47, 69 (nn. 34 and 43), 168, 171, 187 (nn. 2 and 9)
Byron, George Gordon, 118, 119, 123 (nn. 10, 11, and 12)

Calvinism
  and grace, 5–7
  imputed righteousness, 5
  and the outsider, 95
Catholicism, Roman, 2, 10–13
Chambers, R. W., 30 (n. 12)
Charles I, 13, 14, 15, 25, 120
Chesterton, G. K., 183, 188 (n. 31)
Christ, image of, 146–150
Christian Doctrine, The. See De Doctrina Christiana.
Cicero, 18, 60
Coleridge, Samuel Taylor, 164, 167 (n. 28)
Commonwealth of Oceana, 28, 31 (n. 36)
Comus, 50, 73, 81
  ideas of moderation and excess in, 130–139
  themes of virginity and chastity in, 136–138
Congregationalists, 14
Connelly, Marc, 92
Cope, Jackson I., 169, 187 (n. 4)

Daiches, David, 93, 100 (n. 24)
Dalila, 156, 161–163
Dante Alighieri, 7, 11, 60, 92, 103, 107
D'Arcy, M. C., 99 (n. 2)

Dawson, Christopher, 69 (n. 38)
De Civitate Dei (The City of God). See St. Augustine.
De diligendo Deo, 54
De Doctrina Christiana, 7, 19, 22, 25, 30, 31, 34, 35, 45, 66, 68, 69, 70, 71, 87, 93, 100
  all sins included in the Fall, 22
  on biblical interpretation, 35
  Christ died for all men, 77
  meaning of nature, 7
  twofold will denied in God, 87
Defence of the People of England, A, 15, 24, 25, 31 (nn. 26 and 31), 69 (n. 29)
Demosthenes, 18
de Wulf, Maurice, 7, 30 (n. 8)
Divine Comedy, The, 122 (n. 3)
  See also Dante
Doctrine and Discipline of Divorce, 68 (n. 22), 71 (n. 54)
Donne, John, 41
Dostoevski, Fyodor, 103
Duns Scotus, 58

Edward VI, 13
Elizabeth, Queen, 13
Ellul, Jacques, 29 (n. 5)
Empson, William, 76, 91, 99 (n. 1), 119, 123 (n. 14)
Essay on Man, 90
Euripides, 163
Eve. See Adam
Evil, problem of, 101, 104–106, 158–159

Faerie Queene, The, 8, 58, 62, 66, 71 (n. 56), 99 (n. 1),

120, 133, 136, 164 (n. 10), 177
Fall of Man
  both of Adam and Eve, 72
  effect on Adam's descendants, 76, 95
  evolutionary aspects of, 77–79, 85
  includes all sins, 22
  knowledge and, 73–74
  as loss of rational liberty, 79–80
  nature of, 86–89
  paradox of, 78, 80, 106
  See also De Doctrina Christiana
Faust, 21, 119
Faustus, 107, 119
Fifth Monarchy, 15, 42
Fisher, Cardinal, 11
Freedom
  Abdiel on, 28
  earthly and heavenly freedoms, 23–37
  Milton's concept of, 20–23
  political freedom, 23–26
Freud, Sigmund, 174
Frye, Northrop, 23, 31 (n. 24), 81, 87, 93, 99 (n. 3), 100 (nn. 10 and 25), 112, 123 (n. 6), 146, 166 (n. 16), 170, 187 (n. 6)

Genesis, 75, 85, 88, 148, 156
Gilbert, Allan H., 121, 123 (n. 18)
Gilson, Etienne, 3, 29 (n. 4), 70 (n. 45)
Glory
  theme of, 66–67, 107–108
  Satan's search for, 106–113

God the Father, 6, 84, 93
  as self-sufficient transcendence, 108
Goethe, Johann Wolfgang, 119
Grace, 4–8
  prevenient, 79
  rejection of Calvinist emphasis on, 7
  relation to free will, 6–7
  relation to reason, 6–8
Grace, Joan, vii
Great Chain of Being, 54, 108
Green Pastures, 92
Greene, Clarence E., 86, 100 (n. 9)

Haller, William, 42, 166 (n. 18)
Hamilton, Edith, 168, 187 (n. 1)
Hanford, James Holly, 152, 167 (n. 21)
Harding, Davis P., 169, 179, 187 (n. 3), 188 (n. 29)
Harrington, James, 28, 36 (n. 36)
Henry IV of Germany, 11
Henry VIII, 10–13, 21 (n. 15)
Hermes Trismegistus, 125
Hildebrand (St. Gregory VII), 11
Hooker, Richard, 60
Horney, Karen, 111, 123 (n. 5)
Hughes, Merritt Y., viii, 165, 167 (n. 29)
Humanism, background of, 56–61

"Il Penseroso," 124–130, 134, 185–187, 193 (nn. 8–9)
Independents, 15

James I, 40

Job, 21
Johnson, Dr. Samuel, 91
Julius II, Pope, 10

Keats, John, 181
Kelley, Maurice, 123 (n. 7)
King, Edward, 16, 50, 62, 170
  See also "Lycidas"
Knowledge
  dilemma of, in *Paradise Lost*, 84–86
  knowing good through evil, 82
  limitation of, 34, 49
  moderation and, 49, 63
  Paradise Regained as drama of, 32
  Scripture as knowledge, 37–38
  seeking forbidden, 74
Knox, John, 14
Krouse, F. Michael, 155, 167 (nn. 22–25)

"L'Allegro," 124–130, 185–187
Levellers, 15
Lewalski, Barbara Kiefer, 167 (n. 19)
Lewis, C. S., 100 (n. 7), 105, 122 (n. 2), 171, 173, 188 (nn. 15 and 21–24)
Likeliest Means to Remove Hirelings, 36, 68 (n. 15), 70 (n. 44)
Louis XIV of France, 44
Lovejoy, Arthur O., 108, 122 (n. 4)
Loyola, St. Ignatius, 184
Luther, Martin, 2, 6, 10, 12
"Lycidas," 16, 52, 62, 67, 170, 180, 184

religious vision in, 139–146, 160

Machiavelli, Niccolò, 9
Madsen, William G., 60, 71 (n. 58), 146, 166 (n. 17)
Marilla, E. L., 87, 88, 100 (nn. 11, 15, and 16)
Marlowe, Christopher, 119, 123 (n. 13)
Martz, Louis L., 53, 70 (n. 43), 80, 93, 100 (n. 27), 121, 123 (n. 16)
Marx, Karl, 24
Menasseh Ben Israel, 43
Michael, Archangel, 4, 76, 80
Michelangelo, 9
Millenium, Idea of, 39 ff.
Milton, John
  baroque in his poetry, 180–187
  concept of citizenship, 17–18
  concept of right reason, 45–50
  concept of Scripture, 34–39
  concept of trial, 22
  Hellenic influence on, 61–65
  high style in his poetry, 176–179
  as a humanist, 32, 56 ff.
  as an ironic figure, 17
  justification of Providence, 89–99
  as a poet, 168–180
  rejection of natural depravity and predestination, 50
  relation to Independents, 14–15
  relation to Puritanism, 50–61
  relation to scholasticism, 59
  as a Renaissance man, 17
  view of poetry, 174

See also Freedom, Grace, Knowledge
Minturno, Antonio, 165
More, Paul Elmer, 173, 188 (n. 20)
More, Sir Thomas, 8, 9, 12, 57, 59, 70 (n. 47), 71 (nn. 52–53)

Nature
  meaning of primary and secondary laws of, 26–27
  Milton's application of laws of, 25
  unwritten law of, 34
  views of Augustine and Aquinas on, 3
  See also De Doctrina Christiana
Nicolson, Marjorie, 180
Nicomachean Ethics, 62, 71 (n. 61)

Oedipus the King, 116
Of Education, 17, 31 (n. 20), 188 (n. 25)
Of Reformation in England, 16, 30 (n. 15), 44, 69 (n. 26)
"On the Morning of Christ's Nativity," 5, 41, 53, 64, 71 (n. 64)

Paradise Lost
  Christ's redemptive role in, 95–96
  as extension of scriptural knowledge, 39
  glory as a leading theme in, 106–113
  Great Chain of Being in, 54
  the human condition in, 44, 81 ff.
  justification of Providence in, 89 ff.
  as logical structure, 93
  narrative and theological tensions in, 113 ff.
  presentation of evil in, 84, 104
  sense of wonder in, 52
  See also Fall of Man, Knowledge, Nature, Satan
Paradise Regained
  as drama of knowledge, 32
  images of Christ and Satan in, 146 ff.
  Satan of, compared with that of Paradise Lost, 148–150
Parker, William Riley, 167 (n. 27)
Pater, Walter, 71 (n. 60)
Patterson, Frank Allen, viii
Perry, Anne Davidson, 171–172, 188 (n. 16–17)
Peyrère, Isaac de la, 43
Plato, 45–46, 54, 58, 69 (nn. 32–33), 101, 125, 166 (n. 11), 191
  See also Republic, Symposium
Pope, Alexander, 90, 71 (n. 57), 100 (n. 20), 190
Pope, Elizabeth Marie, 147, 167 (nn. 19–20)
Presbyterians, 13–14
Prince, F. T., 179, 188 (n. 30)
Prolusions II, 63, 71 (n. 63)
Prolusions VII, 48, 57, 69 (n. 37), 70 (n. 46)
Protestantism, Radical, 2–14

Puritanism, 24 27, 38
  primacy of will in, 51
  in *Samson Agonistes*, 152–165
Pythagoras, 63

Quennell, Peter, 123 (n. 12)

Rajan, B., 116, 123 (n. 9)
Raleigh, Sir Walter, 89, 71 (n. 57), 100 (n. 18)
Ransom, John Crowe, 170, 187 (n. 7)
Raphael, Archangel, 50, 63, 98, 180
Read, Sir Herbert, 171, 187 (n. 11)
Readie and Easie Way, The, 25, 31 (n. 30)
Reason of Church Government, 16–17, 23, 31 (nn. 19 and 25), 36, 68 (n. 18)
Republic of Plato, 18, 69 (n. 32)
Right Reason, 45–50
Roeder, Ralph, 30 (n. 11)
Roper, William, 12, 30 (n. 14)
Rousseau, Jean Jacques, 82

Salmasius (Claude de Saumaise), 24, 25
Samson Agonistes, 140, 146, 147
  relation to Puritanism, 152–165
  Samson as Nazir in, 153
  tradition of Samson, 154 ff.
Samuel, Irene, 89, 100 (n. 19)
Satan
  analysis of, 101–117
  consistency of characterization, 113–117
  critical views of, 117–122
  as ironic hero, 104–106
  meaning of evil in regard to, 105
  romantic view of, 117–119
  and search for glory, 106–113
  and search for transcendence, 106
Saurat, Denis, 45, 69 (n. 31)
Scaliger, Joseph, 177–178
Scott-Craig, T. S. K., 167 (n. 30)
Second Defence of the English People, A, 16, 31 (nn. 17–18)
Shakespeare, William, 40, 58, 115, 146
  Cymbeline, 40
  Hamlet, 116, 185, 191
  King Lear, 146
  Othello, 114, 115
  Romeo and Juliet, 58, 71 (n. 50)
  Timon of Athens, 146
Shelley, Percy Bysshe, 119
Sidney, Sir Philip, 59, 71 (n. 56)
Socrates, 101, 134
Sophocles, 163
Spenser, Edmund, 8, 58–59, 71 (n. 56), 133, 136, 137, 165 (n. 10), 177
Stein, Arnold, 32–33, 49, 68 (n. 1), 70 (n. 39), 158, 167 (nn. 19 and 26), 170, 187 (n. 5), 190, 193 (n. 2)
Stoll, Elmer Edgar, 122, 123 (n. 20)
Symposium of Plato, 54, 134, 166 (n. 11)
Sypher, Wylie, 184, 188 (n. 32)

Tasso, Torquato, 177

Index

Teilhard de Chardin, Pierre, 78
Tenure of Kings and Magistrates, 26, 31 (n. 32)
Tetrachordon, 26–27, 31 (n. 34), 34, 37, 68 (n. 5)
Thorpe, James, 187 (n. 12)
Tillyard, E. M. W., 88, 100 (n. 14), 113, 123 (n. 8), 166 (n. 14), 179, 184, 188 (nn. 27 and 33), 190, 193 (n. 3)
Treatise of Civil Power, A, 35–36, 68 (nn. 9, 12, and 17), 69 (n. 36), 99, 100 (n. 28)
Tuve, Rosemond, 170, 187 (n. 8)

Utopia of Sir Thomas More, 8, 30 (n. 9), 57, 59, 70 (n. 47), 71 (n. 52)

Viereck, Peter, 192
Virgil, 7, 40, 168, 169, 179

Wain, John, 51, 70 (n. 41)
Waldock, A. J. A., 120, 123 (n. 15)
Werblosky, R. J., 121, 123 (n. 19)
Willey, Basil, 39, 60, 71 (n. 59), 85, 88, 100 (nn. 8, 12, and 17), 190, 193 (n. 1)
Wolfe, Don M., vii
Woodhouse, Arthur S. P., 135, 166 (n. 12)

DATE DUE			
DEC 13, 78			
OCT 12 78			
NOV 1 78			
DEC 1 1 1980			
MAR 3 1 1983			
DEC 4 1986			
NOV 15 1990			
DEC 1 1 1990			
NOV 1 2 1995			

HIGHSMITH 45-220